Teaching Students to
DRIVE THEIR
BRAINS

Donna Wilson   Marcus Conyers

Teaching Students to

DRIVE THEIR

BRAINS

Metacognitive Strategies, Activities, and Lesson Ideas

Alexandria,
Virginia USA

1703 N. Beauregard St. • Alexandria, VA 22311-1714 USA
Phone: 800-933-2723 or 703-578-9600 • Fax: 703-575-5400
Website: www.ascd.org • E-mail: member@ascd.org
Author guidelines: www.ascd.org/write

Deborah S. Delisle, *Executive Director;* Robert D. Clouse, *Managing Director, Digital Content & Publications;* Stefani Roth, *Publisher;* Genny Ostertag, *Director, Content Acquisitions;* Julie Houtz, *Director, Book Editing & Production;* Darcie Russell, *Editor;* Thomas Lytle, *Senior Graphic Designer;* Mike Kalyan, *Manager, Production Services;* Circle Graphics, *Typesetter;* Andrea Wilson, *Senior Production Specialist*

All web links in this book are correct as of the publication date below but may have become inactive or otherwise modified since that time. If you notice a deactivated or changed link, please e-mail books@ascd.org with the words "Link Update" in the subject line. In your message, please specify the web link, the book title, and the page number on which the link appears.

PAPERBACK ISBN: 978-1-4166-2211-6   ASCD product #117002   n6/16
PDF E-BOOK ISBN: 978-1-4166-2213-0; see Books in Print for other formats.
Quantity discounts: 10–49, 10%; 50+, 15%; 1,000+, special discounts (e-mail programteam@ascd.org or call 800-933-2723, ext. 5773, or 703-575-5773). For desk copies, go to www.ascd.org/deskcopy.

Library of Congress Cataloging-in-Publication Data

Names: Wilson, Donna (Psychologist), author. | Conyers, Marcus, author.
Title: Teaching students to drive their brains : metacognitive strategies, activities, and lesson ideas / Donna Wilson and Marcus Conyers.
Description: Alexandria, VA : ASCD, 2016. | Includes bibliographical references and index.
Identifiers: LCCN 2016011184 | ISBN 9781416622116 (pbk.)
Subjects: LCSH: Learning, Psychology of. | Metacognition.
Classification: LCC LB1060 .W554 2016 | DDC 370.15/23–dc23 LC record available at http://lccn.loc.gov/2016011184

25 24 23 22 21 20 19 18 17 16   1 2 3 4 5 6 7 8 9 10 11 12

To educators who teach for and with metacognition and who consistently engage in the process of becoming more effective teachers. And to Bob Sylwester, who has been a colleague and friend for more than 20 years. In 1995, his work, *A Celebration of Neurons,* further opened our eyes to the tremendous potential for improving teaching and learning by applying key aspects of cognitive neuroscience in educational settings. He has been a source of support in our own writing for two decades.

Teaching Students to
DRIVE THEIR
BRAINS

Preface

I'd like to share my professional journey to discover the importance of teaching metacognitive and cognitive skills. I began my career in education as a classroom teacher—eager, enthusiastic, and equipped with the subject matter knowledge and classroom management techniques I learned while earning my undergraduate degree. However, I lacked an understanding of how students learn and how I might teach in ways that would increase their ability to learn. I became a student again in search of those answers. I studied the work of influential educational researchers and theorists, including Robert Sternberg's understanding of intelligence as practical, creative, and analytic, and Reuven Feuerstein's applications of structural cognitive modifiability, the concept that students can become functionally smarter. Later, I had the privilege to engage in post-doctoral study at the late Dr. Feuerstein's institute, the International Center for the Enhancement of Learning Potential in Jerusalem. I found the work of Russian neuropsychologist Alexander Luria equally fascinating. Alongside colleague Sally Church, I began to integrate principles about the brain and school neuropsychology into my work with students who had learning challenges.

After becoming a school psychologist, I returned to the same district, where I worked with 1,000 students to conduct diagnostic assessments, many of which indicated that these struggling students were capable of learning at higher levels but had not been taught the skills and strategies they needed. Acting on these findings, I returned to the classroom, this time coteaching with 2nd grade teachers to provide explicit instruction on strategies students could use to think about their thinking and improve their learning (Wilson, 1996a, 1996b). The positive effect of those lessons on students' academic performance led me to the next phase of my career, pursuing teacher education as a way to share practical applications of the "science of learning" with others. This work has been professionally rewarding, in part because it has given me the opportunity to help fill a gap in teacher education—by applying fascinating research in psychology, neuroscience, and education to provide many practical tools for teaching that support the ways students learn.

- - - - -

A key focus of Marcus's work over the last 35 years in 30 countries has been on cultivating the metacognitive and cognitive skills that drive academic and career performance. He has worked with a broad range of corporate, military, and government organizations, including agencies involved in counterintelligence, law enforcement, and fire and rescue services, as well as college and university students and K–12 educators and administrators. Marcus has presented to audiences around the world, including ministers of education from Ontario, Canada; South Africa; and the United Arab Emirates.

Marcus's professional passion has been for empowering educators with research-based frameworks and strategies for teaching students to become effective thinkers and problem solvers. To this end, he developed the original BrainSMART model for aligning teaching with the science of learning by working with 1,200 K–12 students and tens of thousands of teachers and administrators. He led a three-year initiative with this model for the Florida Department of Education and another with Florida DOE supported by an Annenberg Challenge Grant. The positive results from these initiatives led to our partnership codeveloping curriculum for graduate degree programs with Nova Southeastern University and writing a series of books on applications of mind, brain, and education science.

- - - - -

For the last 16 years, Marcus and I have been on a mission to translate implications of mind, brain, and education research into practical frameworks and strategies for improving classroom practice. With that mission in mind, we have written and published books, given conference presentations, offered live and online professional development to more than 160,000 educators, and codeveloped a graduate studies program with Nova Southeastern University. Teachers and administrators who have studied with us speak enthusiastically about the difference this approach has made for their students and in their own professional practice. One teacher noted that explicit instruction on using metacognition has allowed her students to manage their own learning: "If students know what they know and still need to learn what strategies they need to use [to support their learning], they are much more likely to be successful at school."

In 2001, we introduced the brain-based teaching degree programs at Nova Southeastern University and since then have shared in the excitement of teachers who are energized by the learning gains of students taught to wield metacognitive and cognitive strategies and to become, in the words of one student, "the boss of my brain." We are pleased to share some of the success stories from their classrooms as practical examples of metacognition in action. Teaching these strategies is more important now than ever before.

In March 2016, I was honored to be a presenter at a conference where U.S. Secretary of Education John King introduced the Every Student Succeeds Act (ESSA). A focus of this federal education initiative is to improve both excellence and equity. By empowering *all* students with the metacognitive and cognitive skills they need to achieve at higher levels, schools can more consistently achieve the goals of ESSA. Teaching students to become better thinkers is truly the great leveler in terms of achieving equity and in creating conditions in which all students can flourish.

—Donna Wilson

Acknowledgments

We are inspired by the positive results achieved by educators who have applied our frameworks for putting mind, brain, and learning science into practice in their classrooms and schools. The combination of teaching *for* and *with* metacognition, while keeping brain plasticity front of mind, is especially powerful. We want to thank those teachers whose stories, sample lessons, and perspectives are shared in this book: Tammy Daugherty, Paul Farmer, Mary Driskill, Michael Fitzgerald, Keri Shaver, Regina Cabadaidis, Diane Dahl, Emma Oberlechner, Theresa Dodge, Therese Reder, Kelly Rose, Aaron Rohde, Jess Young, Maureen Ryan, Staci Berry, and Marcy McIver. We also appreciate the work of our highly efficient editor, Karen Bankston, who helped put the finishing touches on our manuscript and guide it through the production process. Thanks to Lorraine Ortner-Blake for creating most of the graphics that illustrate key concepts in this text and to Diane Franklin who interviewed some of the teachers whose stories are shared here. We are grateful for the very productive dialogue we had with Acquisitions Editor Genny Ostertag. This exchange of ideas helped us fine-tune our approach in a way that would meet the needs of the ASCD audience. We also appreciate the care that Editor Darcie Russell and the rest of the publishing team took with our manuscript.

Introduction to Metacognition

What do we want for children and teenagers? What do they need to succeed in school, in their future careers, and in the pursuit of their dreams? Wherever their ambitions lead them, they will benefit from becoming creative problem solvers, analytical thinkers, and effective communicators and collaborators. Guiding students to recognize that they can learn these vital skills and improve them provides a pathway to achieve the goals they set for themselves. Some of the most vital and versatile skillsets we can teach students to develop are the abilities to think about their learning; to be aware of factors that affect their intellectual performance; to know how, when, where, and why to use particular cognitive strategies; and to monitor and adjust their performance of learning tasks.

These abilities fall under the umbrella of *metacognition,* which refers to knowledge about and regulation of one's thinking. At the core of being metacognitive is taking a step back and observing one's thinking, as depicted in Figure 1, which is sometimes called the *reflective process.* Questions that might be asked during this process include What is the problem to be solved? What should I do? How am I doing? How well did I do? What can I do differently and better next time?

The Reflective Process of Metacognition

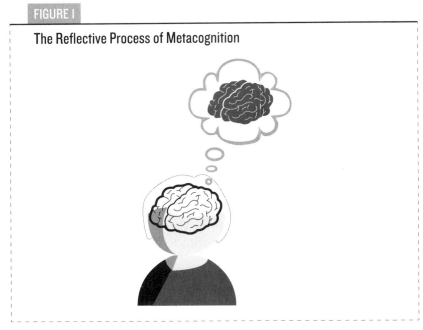

Teaching students to become more metacognitive equips them with skills to "drive their brains" and become self-directed learners. As in driver's education, students need explicit instruction on how to steer their thinking, when they need to slow down and when it's OK to speed up, where they might take shortcuts to get to their learning goals, and when they might benefit from a leisurely road trip along the back roads of knowledge. Many teenagers yearn for their driver's license, but developing the abilities and mindset to take charge of their learning will take them further in life than the keys to any car. And students don't have to wait until their teenage years to take "brain-driving lessons." They can and should start learning about metacognition at an early age and apply it across all core subjects and in life lessons.

Innovative Approach to Teaching Metacognition

This text offers a practitioner-friendly guide for teachers who want to teach both *for* metacognition and *with* metacognition. Teaching for metacognition involves guiding students to become self-reflective, self-directed learners who understand why, how, when, and where to use metacognitive and cognitive strategies; teaching with metacognition entails reflecting on one's teaching approach and the outcomes of classroom practice. Improving student learning is at the center of both goals (see Figure 2).

In contrast to books on this subject that are written primarily for researchers, we take the practical perspective of educators who want to know how the research applies to the everyday tasks of teaching—formulating goals, planning and implementing lessons and activities, self-monitoring while teaching, and learning from experience, with the continual goal of increasing instructional effectiveness. Knowing how important it is for their students to

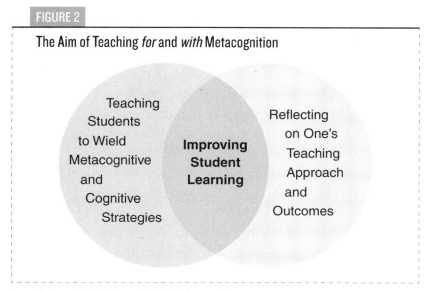

FIGURE 2

The Aim of Teaching *for* and *with* Metacognition

become metacognitive across contexts, teachers will also appreciate the concrete strategies offered here to teach *for* metacognition
throughout the school year.

A second key difference is that our approach is based on our
work with teachers during the last two decades. At the core of our
framework is an understanding of cognitive assets as "workhorses
of the mind," with metacognition as the overseer of that learning
horsepower. For example, think about how crucial it is for students
to use the cognitive asset of selective attention when working on
an important learning task. Teaching students to be metacognitive about directing their attention goes well beyond reminders
to "Pay attention!" Students benefit from explicit instruction on
how to focus their attention, on monitoring how well they are
applying this asset, and on practicing the use of selective attention across contexts in the classroom and in their personal lives.
Metacognition and related cognitive skills are only helpful when
they are used appropriately.

Third, this text relates "big ideas" in education (Wilson &
Conyers, 2013a) to the importance of metacognition in teaching
and learning. We explain the amazing potential of the human brain
through new understandings about neural plasticity—in particular, experience-dependent synaptogenesis and dynamic, malleable
intelligence. We tie together how deploying the cognitive assets
when and how they are needed with metacognition helps students
achieve more of their learning potential and become self-regulated,
independent, and self-directed learners. This approach connects
emerging neuroscience to metacognition in learning.

Fourth, we present metaphors that are beloved by teachers
who use this approach—including the idea of students driving
their brains—to make the complex concept of metacognition easier to understand and apply. We provide a variety of metaphors
and step-by-step suggestions to illustrate the applications of
metacognition and cognitive assets in classroom learning, in students' lives outside of school, and in their future educational and
career pursuits. We share our own stories and real-life examples

from teachers about using these tools and the improvement seen in students' learning.

Throughout this book, we will explore extensive research on how academic achievement is affected when explicit instruction is provided on why, how, and when to use metacognition and cognitive strategies. This research forms the foundation for practical teaching strategies and classroom applications presented in each chapter:

• The sections on teaching with metacognition and specific cognitive strategies in mind offer a concrete approach to planning and delivering lessons in ways that encourage and support self-directed learning. Many of the ideas presented in these sections can be applied across core subjects.

• The sample lessons begin with recommendations on introducing students to the use of the cognitive strategies showcased in each chapter and then lead into an assortment of learning activities for specified grade levels and subject matters. The "extenders" suggest adjustments for younger or older students.

• The Metacognition Checkpoint boxes feature a short list of questions on how students can think more productively about employing the cognitive assets.

• Each chapter concludes with a discussion of how teachers can incorporate the featured cognitive asset into their professional practice, so that they are teaching *for* metacognition as well as *with* metacognition.

Many teachers have told us their classrooms have become more positive, even joyful, as students more often experience those "aha!" moments of learning that come from thinking about their thinking. In addition, educators report that teaching with metacognition has helped transform their classroom practice and attitude about their profession. As one teacher put it, "My students now have a teacher who has the strategies and tools to help them learn to think metacognitively and to teach the 'how' to become successful in school and in their personal lives." The what, why, and how of metacognition is the focus of Chapter 1.

The Case for Teaching *for* and *with* Metacognition

Metacognition is an essential, but often neglected, component of a 21st century education that teaches students *how* to learn. From preschool through high school, the instructional schedule is packed with content lessons with little time for guiding students in developing the metacognitive and cognitive skills that can help them excel in the classroom and in the working world. Although the curriculum and professional development may cover instruction on cognitive strategies, the daily schedule may not provide the explicit teaching and intensive practice students need to learn how, when, where, and why to use these strategies effectively. The assumption seems to be either that children arrive at school naturally equipped with the ability to learn or that they will pick up these skills on their own in the course of learning how to read, write, and do math, science, and social studies—or not. Extending this assumption, students who do not develop thinking and learning abilities on their own are often dismissed as having limited learning potential.

As the research shows, we now know that metacognitive and cognitive abilities are not naturally endowed but can and should be taught and learned. Furthermore, providing this foundation for students through explicit instruction alongside core subject lessons will help develop their abilities to become self-directed learners who are better able to improve their academic performance across the curriculum and effectively transfer and apply what they have learned. As Dunlosky asserts, "teaching students how to learn is as important as teaching them content, because acquiring both the right learning strategies and background knowledge is important—if not essential—for promoting lifelong learning" (2013, pp. 12–13).

Defining Metacognition

Metacognition involves thinking about one's thinking, or cognition, with the goal of enhancing learning. Much of the educational theory and research surrounding metacognition is based on the work of developmental psychologist John Flavell, who applied this terminology in describing the management of information-processing activities that occur during *cognitive transactions*. "Metacognition refers, among other things, to the active monitoring and consequent regulation and orchestration of these processes . . . usually in service of some concrete goal or objective" (1976, p. 232). More simply put, metacognition involves being knowledgeable about and in control of one's cognitive abilities:

> Metacognitive knowledge includes knowledge about oneself as a learner and the factors that might impact performance, knowledge about strategies, and knowledge about when and why to use strategies. Metacognitive regulation is the monitoring of one's cognition and includes planning activities, awareness of comprehension and task performance, and evaluation of the efficacy of monitoring processes and strategies. (Lai, 2011, p. 2)

A student uses metacognition when she reads an unfamiliar word and decides to use two strategies she has learned to puzzle out a word's meaning—breaking it down into components and looking for contextual clues. After she checks her guess against the glossary in the textbook, she thinks, "I was fairly close, and this was good practice. I might run across words I don't know when I take the SAT, and I won't be able to look those up." Another student studying for a test is being metacognitive when he consciously uses several memory strategies and compares them to determine which one seems to work the best for enhancing recall. The goal of teaching students to be metacognitive is to guide them to consciously, and with increasing independence, recognize when and how to employ cognitive strategies that work best for them across various situations.

Hand in hand with teaching metacognition is explicit instruction on the use of these cognitive strategies, or *cognitive assets*. We use the term *assets* to convey that these abilities are extremely valuable and can be enhanced with practice and regular use. Throughout this text, we will present a variety of cognitive assets—specific tools that can be used to complete tasks and to transfer learning across a variety of contexts. Students employ these cognitive assets across core content to

- Maintain an outlook of practical optimism about their learning performance,

- Set learning goals and plan to achieve them,

- Focus their selective attention and optimize working memory,

- Monitor their learning progress, and

- Apply their learning experiences across core subjects and in their personal lives.

Historically, educators focused on the *cognitive deficits* that students bring to learning tasks, which were regarded as relatively fixed and used to explain poor academic performance. By changing our focus to *cognitive assets,* we aim to communicate that strategies for improving learning performance can be taught, learned, and improved with practice. Refocusing on strengths rather than deficits leads to a more incremental view of learning, sometimes referred to as a *growth mindset* (Dweck, 2006) and *dynamic intelligence.*

Viewing learning as an incremental process applies to virtually all students, whatever their performance levels. In the United States, instruction in higher-order thinking processes has often been reserved for students identified as gifted. Of course, high-performing students benefit from learning how to wield metacognitive and cognitive strategies—and so do their peers, including students with learning challenges. In fact, teaching struggling learners how, when, and why to use these strategies may help them catch up in academic performance and recognize that they can succeed in achieving learning goals with hard work and persistent effort. After teaching students with moderate to severe disabilities how to use cognitive skills as part of instruction on core subject lessons, California middle school teacher Paul Farmer reported that "the accumulation of small incremental changes over time might result in measurable and meaningful functional outcomes" (personal correspondence, January 10, 2013).

The cognitive assets make up a toolbox of versatile thinking tools that can be taught—but not in isolation from metacognition. Students must learn how to use metacognition to know how and when to use these assets to successfully master learning and problem-solving challenges, both inside and outside the classroom, and to assess how well they are using these strategies. A variety of cognitive assets are presented in the following chapters. Paired with instruction on when and how to use these assets— to apply a metacognitive approach—students can learn to wield powerful tools that can help them in school and life contexts, from taking tests to maintaining healthy and positive relationships with friends and family.

The use of metacognition and cognitive strategies engages two levels of thinking. The first level involves applying a cognitive strategy to solve a problem; the second involves using metacognition to select and monitor the effectiveness of that strategy. Hattie describes metacognition as "higher order thinking, which involves active control over the cognitive process engaged in learning" (2009, p. 188). Teaching students to be metacognitive involves building their knowledge about cognition and their ability to take charge of their brainpower; enhancing their understanding of how, why, and when to use the cognitive assets that are essential in learning how to learn; and assessing how well they are using cognitive assets and what they might do to improve their learning.

Here are several other terms associated with metacognition:

• *Executive function* describes the brain processes and mental faculties involved in goal setting, planning and execution, reasoning, problem solving, working memory, and organization.

• *Higher-order thinking,* sometimes called *critical thinking,* generally refers to going beyond the rote memorization of facts to skills such as analyzing, synthesizing, and transferring knowledge to other applications.

• *Self-regulation* and *self-directed learning* are accomplished by guiding students to recognize that they are in charge of their emotions, thoughts, and actions, and by equipping them with strategies and skills to steer their feelings, thinking, and behaviors in positive and productive directions.

• *Mindfulness* refers to focusing one's consciousness on current feelings, thoughts, and sensations. By being mindful of their emotional state, for example, teachers and students can more effectively steer their feelings and thoughts in a more positive, "can-do" direction (see Chapter 3).

The center of these cognitive functions in the brain is the prefrontal cortex, located directly behind the forehead. Goldberg describes the prefrontal cortex as the brain's "chief executive officer" for its role in "forming goals and objectives and then in devising plans of action required to obtain these goals. It selects the cognitive skills required to complete the plans, coordinates these skills, and applies them in correct order" (2009, p. 23). More recent research (Fleming, 2014) also identifies this area of the brain—specifically the anterior prefrontal cortex—as the center of metacognition.

Executive function, higher-order thinking, and self-regulation can all be improved over time using metacognition. If these cognitive functions and assets perform as musicians in the orchestra of learning, then metacognition is the conductor. The conductor chooses which works to perform, leads the musicians through intensive practice, maintains the tempo, directs various sections to take the lead at times, and reviews the performance to pinpoint where fine-tuning may be needed. In the same way, by developing our metacognitive capacities, we can better direct our attention to the learning task at hand, choose which cognitive assets are needed for the task, monitor our performance, and identify how we might improve our learning.

Because the concepts of metacognition and executive function can seem quite abstract, using phrases like "driving your brain" or identifying metacognition as the conductor of the orchestra of learning can help make these ideas more concrete and practical for students. And it is certainly worth the effort to teach students how they can take charge of their learning and, by monitoring and improving their use of the cognitive assets, make steady gains in learning.

Why Teach for Metacognition?

The traditional emphasis on subject matter knowledge—with little or no time allotted to teach metacognitive and cognitive strategies—may not adequately prepare students for college and career. A report from the National Research Council on "Education for Life and Work" (Pellegrino & Hilton, 2012) identifies three domains of 21st century competencies—cognitive (thinking and reasoning), intrapersonal (regulating one's behaviors and emotions to achieve goals), and interpersonal (relating to others and understanding others' points of view)—that are supported by many of the cognitive assets featured in this text.

No longer is it enough to demonstrate an understanding of the curriculum or to know how to use basic learning skills. Rather, students must be able to deploy content knowledge and apply thinking strategies appropriately on their own in new learning situations. In short, they may benefit from "the full range of metacognitive strategies ... to monitor and direct their thinking and learning" (National Governors Association Center for Best Practices & Council of Chief State School Officers, 2010a, p. 4). As Billings and Roberts note in *Educational Leadership,* the Common Core State Standards emphasize the development of skills to support independent learning and college and career readiness and "assume that teachers are ultimately teaching students to think—the most difficult and important literacy skill of all" (2012/2013, p. 72). Metacognition is at the heart of our approach to learning and teaching students to think.

Instructional strategies that emphasize metacognition in supporting new standards have a solid record of success, according to educational research. In a meta-analysis of 91 studies, Wang, Haertel, and Walberg (1993) determined that metacognition is the number one shared characteristic of high academic achievers. On a more recent list of 150 factors that influence student achievement, metacognitive strategies were ranked 15th; by comparison, student socioeconomic status (which is often assumed to be a major influence on students' learning potential) was ranked 45th (Hattie, 2012). "Strong learners can explain which strategies they used to solve a problem and why, while less competent students monitor their own thinking sporadically and ineffectively and offer incomplete explanations" (Pellegrino & Hilton, 2012, p. 92). The encouraging conclusion is that the gap between high achievers and struggling students can be closed by guiding the latter to develop a metacognitive approach to learning.

Other research supports the importance of metacognition for learning across contexts and provides a wide body of evidence that metacognitive strategies can be taught and learned (Bransford, Brown, & Cocking, 2000; Efklides & Misailidi, 2010; Hacker, Dunlosky, & Graesser, 2009; Hartman, 2002; Lai, 2011; Winne & Azevedo, 2014). A 2014 study by Veenman and colleagues suggests that the ability to apply a metacognitive approach to learning may account for some 40 percent of the variation in academic achievement across a range of outcomes. Lai (2011) reports on classroom research in which teachers included explicit instruction on the use of metacognition alongside math lessons, stating that 8th graders who learned about metacognition outperformed peers in a comparison group in their abilities to interpret graphs, explain math concepts and reasoning, and transfer math knowledge to other applications. In fact, extensive research on the explicit teaching of metacognitive and cognitive strategies indicates that when students are taught how to learn and think, they can achieve at higher academic levels (Allington, 2011; Anderman & Anderman, 2009; Cawelti, 2004; Good & Brophy, 2008; Hartman, 2010; Hattie, 2009; Marzano, 2007; Marzano & Pickering, 2011).

Despite the wealth of research on the importance of teaching metacognition, educational practice in the United States continues to focus almost exclusively on content knowledge. Baker (2013) writes that "metacognitive strategies instruction is still not commonly observed in most primary and secondary classrooms, and interviews with teachers have revealed limited knowledge about metacognition and how to foster it." A major study of lessons taught in hundreds of elementary classrooms found that, on average, 5th graders received 500 percent more instruction on basic skills than on metacognition and higher-order thinking skills; the ratio for 1st and 3rd graders was 10:1 (Pianta, Belsky, Houts, & Morrison, 2007).

These findings are especially discouraging given that metacognition is at the heart of learning. The Educational Psychology Committee of the American Psychological Association formally defines *learning* as creating meaningful representations of knowledge through internally mediated processes including self-awareness, self-questioning, self-monitoring, and self-regulation (APA Division 15 Committee on Learner-centered Teacher Education for the 21st Century, 1995). These are the same processes at the core of metacognition, but this approach to learning is not a birthright. Many students do not come to school ready to achieve at high levels. The academic performance of most children and teenagers, whatever their current levels of achievement, can be enhanced by explicit instruction on the use of metacognitive and cognitive strategies. Receiving this instruction can help students to acquire the knowledge and skills they need to succeed as learners in the 21st century and to develop "the cogent reasoning and use of evidence that is essential to both private deliberation and responsible citizenship in a democratic republic" (National Governors Association Center for Best Practices & Council of Chief State School Officers, 2010a, p. 3).

Becoming more metacognitive helps learners of all ages—children, teenagers, and adults—proactively determine what they know and what they need to know in order to succeed. A metacognitive mindset toward learning has also been linked to increasing motivation because students who are taught to use these thinking strategies are more confident about their academic abilities and understand that persistence in the sometimes hard work of learning will pay off.

Teachers who have earned their graduate degrees in the programs we codeveloped with Nova Southeastern University (NSU) call metacognition the gift that keeps on giving—to their students and in their own professional practice and personal lives. In a survey of these teachers regarding what they learned about metacognition in their graduate studies, 88 percent of respondents agreed that they are better equipped to teach their students how to be better thinkers, and 83 percent agreed that their students have developed a better understanding of how to improve their own learning (Harman & Germuth, 2012). In an ethnographic study of program graduates, a kindergarten teacher commented that teaching her students to think about their thinking has helped them to regulate their behavior and choices:

> "Teaching them how to think about multiple ways to solve problems has helped students become more focused, calmer, problem-solve more, and better at working out things between themselves versus needing to get the teacher involved," she said. This way of teaching, she believes, "helps with behavior management" and has resulted in a better classroom climate where her students "have more respect for one another . . . work in harmony more, and work things out more than putting it back on the teacher." (Germuth, 2012, pp. 12–13)

Another NSU graduate who teaches English as a second language to elementary students credited explicit instruction on the use of metacognitive and cognitive strategies as one factor in the significant decrease in the rate of students who did not meet state reading comprehension strategies, from 72 percent at the beginning of the school year to 17 percent near the end of the year. Regarding the outcome of becoming more metacognitive in her own practice, this teacher noted that "I was able to be more consistent about how and when to use strategies and recognize what works for different kids, and this shows up in [test] scores" (Germuth, 2012, p. 17).

These teachers' experiences are consistent with the research connecting instruction on the use of metacognition and cognitive strategies to learning gains. Students who succeed academically have learned to think effectively and independently. They employ crucial fundamental skills, such as keeping their workspace organized, completing tasks on schedule, making a plan for learning, monitoring their learning path, and recognizing when it might be useful to change course. Students who succeed academically have been taught to be metacognitive and therefore think effectively and independently and do not rely on their teacher to initiate learning tasks and monitor their progress. In comparison, students who tend to have lower academic performance have not been taught about cognitive assets or how to manage their learning and therefore experience more setbacks, become discouraged and disengaged from learning, and may be responsible for many classroom management issues. Thus, teaching for and with metacognition benefits individual learners and helps to foster a more positive and productive learning environment.

Teaching with Metacognition in Mind: Think Aloud to Model Metacognition

As the lead learner in your classroom, you can make the concept of metacognition more concrete for students by demonstrating it in action across subject lessons. By thinking aloud about the meaning of unfamiliar words and correcting deliberate mistakes in math calculations, for example, you can show students how useful it is to think about your thinking and how metacognition can be applied across contexts in school and outside the classroom. These think-alouds also convey the message to students that everyone— even the teacher—can learn from their mistakes and benefit from thinking about how they learn and how they might improve their learning. This approach recasts missteps from evidence of failure to opportunities to learn and improve. By thinking aloud and using the vocabulary of metacognition, you can effectively model the type of metacognitive discourse that students can employ individually and in small and large groups.

Introducing Metacognition and Cognitive Assets

To help introduce metacognition and cognitive assets to students, we suggest using the following ideas as starting points. These ideas can be adapted for use with students across grade levels and to reflect the lesson content of diverse subjects.

Introduce the terminology, define it, and use it often.
Explicit instruction on the use of metacognition, which can be
simply defined as "thinking about your thinking as a pathway
to better learning," is appropriate and useful for all students.
Children as young as 3 years old can think about their thinking at
basic levels and use simple metacognitive strategies to regulate
their thinking and behaviors (Kuhn, 2000; Lai, 2011). Georgia
teacher Mary Driskill introduces 2nd graders to the term *metacognition* by explaining that thinking about our thinking "helps
us to understand why we're coming up with the answers that we
do." It's a big word for young students, she acknowledges, but
helps drive home the message that they can get smarter by setting
learning goals and working hard to achieve them. At the same
time, don't assume older students are familiar with the concept of
thinking about their thinking to improve learning. Idaho teacher
Michael Fitzgerald (personal conversation, April 25, 2015) says
the concept of metacognition is new to many of the high school
seniors studying Shakespeare in his English class. "I tell them,
'Doing school successfully is not just about the subject matter. It's
about the thinking skills you're learning and how you learn to use
your mind metacognitively.'"

Begin with an explicit lesson on metacognition, including what it is and how students can use it across all domains to
improve their learning. Then incorporate the use of metacognition into core lessons often—perhaps three or four times a day
throughout the first week—and touch on it regularly thereafter.
We suggest introducing one new cognitive asset per week, as your
instructional calendar permits, and tying each new asset into a
metacognitive approach to learning to monitor implementation
and regular use. In this way, each cognitive asset takes center stage
for a week and then is woven into ongoing reminders and opportunities to apply metacognitive and cognitive strategies to specific
lessons and activities. As Pellegrino and Hilton summarize the
research on teaching metacognition, "Sustained instruction and
effort are necessary to develop expertise in problem solving and

metacognition; there is no simple way to achieve competence without time, effort, motivation, and informative feedback" (2012, p. 10). Following an introduction on the importance of applying metacognition to learning, "the teaching of metacognitive skills is often best accomplished in specific content areas since the ability to monitor one's understanding is closely tied to domain-specific knowledge and expertise" (p. 92).

Use metaphors to explain and explore how metacognition works and how students can benefit from becoming more metacognitive. The following "brain car" lesson and the metaphor of driving your brain make the concept of metacognition more concrete and practical for students.

Catch students being metacognitive, perhaps when they reflect on their individual learning or engage in metacognitive discourse in group activities, and celebrate it in small or large groups as a way to underscore the many ways this approach to learning comes in handy.

Lead discussions encouraging students to share examples of how metacognition can be employed inside and outside the classrooms. When coauthor Donna Wilson teaches metacognition to younger students, she encourages them to share how their parents might use metacognition at work. High school students could think about applying metacognition in their summer jobs and personal interactions with friends and family.

Lesson: Driving Brain Cars

Level: Upper Elementary

Introduce the concept. The "driving your brain" metaphor is a concrete and engaging way to introduce students to the concept of taking charge of their learning. In this sample lesson with elementary students, the teacher introduces the word *cognition* as "a scientific term for something we do all the time—think!" She continues, "*Metacognition* is thinking about your thinking in ways that can help you become a better learner." The teacher shares several examples of metacognition, such as thinking about concentrating on a lesson rather than being distracted by noises in the hallway or by other students, thinking about all the memory strategies the class is learning and which one has worked best for you, thinking about developing a plan to complete a project and then checking off each step in the plan to complete the project on time, and thinking about how you did on a test and what you might do differently next time to get a better grade. She asks students to share examples of meta-cognition inside and outside school and writes their suggestions on the board: thinking about the best ways to research a topic for a paper, thinking about how to organize a book report, making a plan to save money for a new bike and carrying it out, and coming up with fun things to do with siblings and parents on family nights. It is a diverse list and provides many opportunities to discuss the varied aspects of metacognition in planning, implementing, and evaluating outcomes.

Activity. Next, the teacher shares the image of the brain cars (see Figure 1.1) and introduces the metaphor of "driving your brain." By becoming more metacognitive, she explains, you

FIGURE 1.1

Brain Cars

can drive your brain to better learning. She provides a couple examples of steering clear of distractions and knowing when you need to back up to make sure you understand the lesson and when you can speed on to the next idea. The teacher passes out sheets with the brain car and asks students to add a label about how they can drive their brains to better learning with metacognition. Again, their ideas are diverse and creative. One student draws a TV with a red X over it and adds a label that he needs to "drive past video games until my homework is done." Another writes, "When I look up the right answers and write them next to the ones I missed on a test, I am driving my brain to an *A*!" A third student, remembering a recommendation the teacher has repeated often, writes, "Practice, practice, practice makes me the best brain driver!" One student embellishes her brain car to show it speeding so fast that flames are shooting out the back. Another adds a long and winding road around the car and notes, "My brain car is going far."

Transfer the learning. The teacher collects the brain cars and displays them around the room. Throughout the week, she mentions metacognition and the brain cars in lessons: "Let's be metacognitive about planning this science experiment. What are we trying to figure out, and what evidence should we be collecting?" "Let's put our brain cars in reverse and think if there's another way to solve this math problem." "How do you think the first settlers in our state used metacognition in deciding where to build their homes?" Soon the students are following her lead. When she asks a student how he figured out the meaning of an unfamiliar word, he replies, "I thought about what I was thinking about the rest of the sentence and how that word might fit." The teacher hears another student in a reading circle remark about a character: "If she would only be more metacognitive, she wouldn't make the same mistake again and again!" When the teacher asks the class "What makes the best brain car driver?" the students often respond in unison, "Practice, practice, practice!"

Extenders. Using the brain car metaphor to teach students about metacognition is effective even for very young children, who might enjoy adding noises and motions as reminders for speeding along, stepping on the brakes, and steering clear of obstacles to learning. It can also be an effective extended metaphor for middle school and high school students, especially if they are just being introduced to the concept of taking charge of their learning by practicing metacognition. A question for older students might be "Many of you are excited about the prospects of getting your driver's license. But what are the benefits of learning to drive your brain?"

Keri Shaver, who works with individual high schoolers online through Florida Virtual School, says a metacognitive approach to learning offers students a variety of thinking strategies to keep trying until the light bulb comes on. "Their confidence increases once they realize they have potential to learn and achieve. The cognitive assets I found especially useful had to do with time management. I was able to use those as strategies to keep them on schedule," she says. "I could say, 'You want to get this class done by December, correct? And how many weeks is that?' I put the ownership in their hands."

Metacognition Checkpoint

Encourage students to take a metacognitive approach to learning by asking themselves questions like these:

- How can metacognition help me learn better?
- Am I driving my brain right now, or is my brain on autopilot and steering away from learning?
- In thinking about how I studied for this test, are there things I can do to improve my study habits?
- Are there other ways to think about this problem and possible ways to solve it?

Metacognition in Your Professional Practice

Emphasizing the "language of learning"—or referring regularly to metacognition and the cognitive assets to remind students to think about their thinking—pays the dividend of reinforcing the positive aspects of being metacognitive about your teaching practice.

- In planning lessons, ask yourself, What are the most important elements of this lesson? Where might students encounter difficulties? How can I measure how effectively students have learned them? How can I tie this new content to their prior knowledge? Which metacognitive strategies and cognitive assets should I remind students to activate to make the most of this learning?

- While engaged in the lesson, monitor learning with questions like these: Is this lesson going as I planned? If not, what is leading us off course? Are we proceeding at the right pace? How can I keep students who have demonstrated their understanding of this new content engaged and moving forward, while providing additional practice for other students who are still working to learn? Is there any content that seems confusing or unclear? What unexpected connections are students making, and how can we capitalize on that?

- In evaluating outcomes, review these issues: Do the assessments demonstrate that students have mastered this new content? Do some students need additional support or reviews? What might I do differently the next time I teach this lesson? What was unexpected, in both positive and challenging ways? Can we apply this new knowledge to other subjects and build on the learning?

Questions like these are at the heart of teaching with metacognition, as is continually monitoring instructional effectiveness and learner engagement. Using questions will help the "learning brains" in your classroom—those of your students and your own!—focus productively on the task at hand.

2

Metacognition and the Learning Brain

Over time, when students use metacognitive and cognitive strategies to improve academic performance, they are actually building their brainpower. Research has established that learning changes the structure and function of the brain (Bransford, Brown, & Cocking, 2000; Hinton, Fischer, & Glennon, 2012). Neuronal connections form in response to the thoughts, actions, and sensory input that occur during learning through a process known as *synaptogenesis*. Reinforcing knowledge and skill development through repetition and practice strengthens those connections. Thus, becoming more metacognitive about one's academic and personal pursuits can help make the most of this *neural plasticity—* the brain's capacity to change and grow and to become functionally smarter.

One form of neural plasticity is termed *experience dependent synaptogenesis*, the process by which new synapses form as a result of our experiences and interactions with our environment. "In experience-dependent development, individual differ-

24

ences in brain development depend on the idiosyncratic experiences that are encountered across the life span. . . . Experience-dependent brain development is a source of enduring plasticity and adaptability to the demands of everyday life." (Shonkoff & Phillips, 2000, p. 190). *Repeated* experiences and environmental stimuli—such as learning and applying new knowledge over time—strengthen synaptic connections, while synapses formed from experiences that are *not repeated* are lost in a process known as pruning. Because no two people have exactly the same experiences throughout life, experience-dependent synaptogenesis is a mechanism that makes each of our brains unique.

Neuroscientists have found evidence of this form of synaptic development at work in brain scans of medical students studying for exams, musicians engaged in intensive practice, and cab drivers learning to navigate the labyrinth of London (Draganski et al., 2006; Glaser & Schlaug, 2003; Woollett & Maguire, 2011). This research has detected visible changes in areas of the brain associated with memory, spatial reasoning, and problem solving, and supports a conceptualization of intelligence as malleable and dynamic. This view stands in contrast to previously widespread perceptions of fixed intelligence—the idea that we are born with a predetermined level of intellectual capacity and that no amount of education can move the dial. But because there is no expiration date on a healthy brain's plasticity, nearly everyone—regardless of age—has the potential to expand his or her knowledge and develop new skills. For students, using metacognitive and cognitive strategies is like adding high-octane fuel to their brain cars to help optimize the synaptic connections the brain forms in response to learning.

Metacognition is about having the *will* to think effectively and the *skill* of being able to think about one's thinking with the goal of steadily improving learning and taking advantage of brain plasticity. Students are more motivated to take charge of their learning when they understand the amazing potential of their brains to become functionally smarter. Explicit instruction on brain plasticity provides the *why* and the *how* for students to become aware that learning changes their brains and that they can regulate those processes through the increasingly sophisticated use of metacognition and supporting cognitive assets (see Figure 2.1).

To share this message with his students, Idaho teacher Michael Fitzgerald draws a diagram of a neuron on the chalkboard and shows how synapses fire and form connections to other neurons in response to new experiences and learning. "I tell them, 'There are things in life you're not in charge of, but you are in

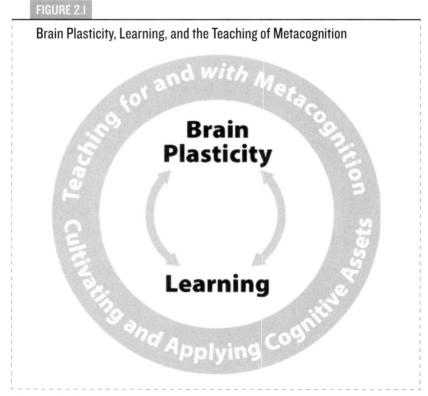

FIGURE 2.1

Brain Plasticity, Learning, and the Teaching of Metacognition charge of you. When you accept that, your brain changes. And every time your brain changes, you grow,'" he says. "That can be very empowering, but it also challenges them to take charge of their learning."

Mr. Fitzgerald teaches English at Eagle Academy, a public charter school created as an alternative high school for at-risk youth in Boise. His teaching incorporates the ideas that students can become progressively smarter by thinking about their thinking. These concepts are new to many of Mr. Fitzgerald's students and pave the way for cognitive and metacognitive strategies that he explicitly introduces and models as a way "to successfully do school." At a more basic level, he says, learning about brain plasticity and metacognition helps to answer a perennial question: "Why do we need to learn this?"

"Especially with the push toward more standardized testing, it seems that students are thinking more and more, 'I just have to learn these facts because I'm told it's important.' But they don't see how it matters, and furthermore, they think school is a waste of their time," Mr. Fitzgerald says. "I tell them Shakespeare is a great writer, but a more fundamental reason why we study Shakespeare is that it helps us develop our minds."

As students read and discuss Shakespeare's plays and other literature, Mr. Fitzgerald also emphasizes the usefulness of learning to establish their clear intent in undertaking a project for class (a cognitive asset we will discuss in Chapter 4), to direct their selective attention (see Chapter 5), and to develop memory strategies to enhance "how much you can hold in your brain."

"Knowing how to read Shakespeare can help you understand how to read directions and other complex text," he says. "When you study calculus, you are learning how to think systemically about solving a problem. These are the fundamental skills of being human."

"Metacognition—learning to monitor and regulate their thoughts—that's not something these students have ever been taught," Mr. Fitzgerald adds. "That's by and large because schools don't teach them these things because teachers don't know about those things. Ultimately, English and math and other subjects are not as important as the thinking skills you're learning and how you learn to use your mind metacognitively."

This message strikes a chord with students of all ages. It's a *big* concept for the 3- to 6-year-olds in Regina Cabadaidis's preK/K class at S.D. Spady Elementary School in Delray Beach, Florida. *Metacognition* is one of the first words she writes on the white board as the school year begins. Ms. Cabadaidis emphasizes using their brains in terms of self-regulation in their daily lives, offering practical examples of taking charge of getting ready for school on time and considering the consequences for not following directions. The children embrace the idea of taking charge of their thinking, sharing it with their parents, and spontaneously relating what they are learning to storybook characters when their teacher reads aloud in class, such as the classic *Tale of Peter Rabbit*.

"You know the story—the mother rabbit dresses up all of her children and tells them not to go into Mr. McGregor's farm. Peter Rabbit goes anyway," Ms. Cabadaidis says. "The children got very excited at this part, saying, 'Peter Rabbit didn't have metacognition. He went into Mr. McGregor's farm when his mother told him not to, and he got into a lot of trouble! He lost the brass buttons to his new blue coat!' "

Teaching Metacognition with the Learning Brain in Mind

Advances in the science of brain plasticity show that virtually all students can improve their academic performance when their schooling is characterized by effective teaching approaches, plentiful opportunities for practice and relearning when warranted, and explicit instruction on metacognitive and cognitive strategies that allow them to become self-directed learners. Under these conditions and with these supports, struggling readers can succeed, and students who "can't do math" can learn to proficiently "make sense of problems and persevere in solving them" and transfer their skills "to solve problems arising in everyday life, society, and the workplace" (National Governors Association Center for Best Practices & Council of Chief State School Officers, 2010b, pp. 6–7). The new view of *learning potential* replaces the hopeless conclusion that a student can't learn a lesson with the more hopeful and actionable deduction that he or she hasn't learned it *yet.*

Learning can be envisioned as taking place across three phases:

1. *Input,* where learners identify what they need to know and gather the information needed for successful outcomes;

2. *Processing,* the stage in which learners examine, analyze, and elaborate on the information gathered in the input phase; and

3. *Output,* where learners communicate, apply, and demonstrate their newly developed knowledge and skills (Wilson & Conyers, 2011b).

Students can be guided to apply a metacognitive approach and useful cognitive assets along each of these phases of learning and to pinpoint where breakdowns in learning may occur. For example, a student who usually enjoys writing is having a hard time with an essay. When she steps back to analyze the problem, she realizes she needs to go back to the input phase and gather additional information. Another student demonstrates mastery of new math concepts in class and on homework but tends to do poorly on tests. His grades improve after a series of lessons on strategies to prepare for tests, read directions carefully, and employ stress reduction techniques so that his brain is "de-stressed and test-ready." Discussing learning as a process that occurs in phases offers students a useful framework for applying a metacognitive approach to their schoolwork.

Florida teacher Tammy Daugherty says equipping students with strategies to think about their learning is especially effective with those who had previously struggled with learning. Teaching for metacognition supports differentiated instruction, providing individual students with cognitive tools to enhance their strengths and overcome learning challenges, she notes. "I no longer think of myself as the person who's teaching at the kids. I'm the facilitator, and the kids are becoming independent learners using their skills," Ms. Daugherty adds. "It just makes my classroom run smoother."

Providing Instruction on Metacognition and the Learning Brain

To help provide instruction on using metacognition to support students' learning brains, we suggest using the following ideas:

Introduce the concept of brain plasticity with a question to begin a discussion: Who can share an example of something that used to be difficult for you to do but has become easier after you practiced it? Examples may include reading, riding a bike, playing a musical instrument, speaking a nonnative language, or participating in a sport.

Explain that as students learned and practiced these new skills, their brains changed. Reading is much easier now because their brains recognize the words they have learned and stored in long-term memory. Their brains have also stored strategies for figuring out the meaning of unfamiliar words based on context and similarities to other words they know. The same is true for physical skills: the parts of their brains that control large and small motor skills have learned how to play a musical piece or dribble a basketball so these actions become much more automatic.

Share with students a concept that may be new to them. Just because they don't know something or aren't good at something doesn't mean students can't learn it and get better— all thanks to their malleable brains. Just as they learned other skills, sometimes through a great deal of practice and coaching, they can learn school subjects that may have been difficult for them in the past.

Note that for many skills, learning gets easier as you progress because you can build on what you already know. That's why the class often begins a new unit of study by reviewing what students may have learned previously about the topic.

Emphasize that monitoring their learning and thinking about ways to improve their learning can help drive changeable brains to learning success.

Lesson: Building a Group Brain

Level: Lower Elementary

Texas teacher Diane Dahl teaches 2nd graders about the brain during the first week of school. They learn what *neurons, axons,* and *dendrites* are and how connections in the brain create learning. Mrs. Dahl emphasizes that each child has an amazing, unique brain and that through effort and practice, every student will learn and remember a lot during the year.

Next, Mrs. Dahl tells students that when we learn, it is important to connect new information with something we already know. She gives a few examples and then tells students they will be making a model of their class's brain and what they are thinking and learning, using pipe cleaners and sticky notes. The lesson uses these steps:

1. Each student gets three pipe cleaners to twist together to represent axons. Remind them to leave the ends untwisted to represent the dendrites.

2. Students work together to build the class brain structure, connecting all the axons and dendrites, with guidance from the teacher. The structure represents the class's brain at the beginning of the school year.

3. Throughout the school year, students create and add new axons and dendrites to the brain, labeled with sticky notes on new concepts they have learned. The notes are folded and stapled over the pipe cleaners.

The following are Mrs. Dahl's tips for success:

• As the year progresses, the brain model gets more complicated, and it's more difficult for 2nd graders to add new connections (this might not be an issue for older students). At some point, I take over making the new connections.

• I write the labels so we can all keep track of the new learning that is added to the brain, using both sides of the label so it can be seen from more than one vantage point as the structure becomes more elaborate.

• We suspend the brain from the ceiling—low enough that students can interact with it and read the labels. We choose a location away from busy traffic areas.

• Whenever possible, we connect new learning with previous lessons. For example, when we studied China, students made a connection about the invention of paper to an earlier lesson on Sequoyah, who invented a writing system for the Cherokee people. When students learned about the Mississippi River, they connected knowledge about the length of the waterway to other rivers around the world; they learned about the Amazon and Yellow rivers earlier in the year and the Nile in 1st grade.

"This model is a nice visual representation of our class's 'group' brain and what we are learning," Mrs. Dahl says. "It illustrates metacognition as we use our brain model throughout the year to think about our thinking and learning over time. Students are very excited at the prospect of adding to our brain 'structure' throughout the year, and we periodically gather around the brain to reflect on new learning and how it connects to what the students already know."

Extender. Lessons on strategies to build on what students already know about a new topic of study offer a practical application for middle school classes as a group project or independent study. For example, in the classic K-W-L strategy (Ogle, 1986), students fill in a three-column chart. In the first two columns, students write What I Know about the subject and What I Want to Know. This exercise helps to personalize the lesson by guiding each student to think about his or her unique past experiences with the topic and specific interests in learning more. When the lesson is complete, students return to the chart to complete the third column, What I Learned. This review offers a valuable metacognitive step and reinforces the connection between existing and new knowledge.

Lesson: Applying the IPO Model to Independent Study

Level: Middle School Science

Before launching an independent study project in which students will research and develop a presentation on the science topic of their choice, the teacher introduces the input, processing, and output (IPO) model to guide them through three phases of learning that will take place as they work on their projects:

Input. Students begin their projects by formulating a clear statement of what they plan to achieve and then gather information from multiple reliable sources.

Processing. The next phase involves reviewing and analyzing the information gathered during the input phase and adapting and applying it to create the project, whether students are working on a graphical depiction, a model, or an experiment. As they process the information, they may need to return to the input phase and track down additional data.

Output. During this final phase, students complete and deliver their project. The teacher emphasizes that if students have done their work adequately in the first two phases, the output phase will be much easier and more successful.

The teacher explains that though this model may seem new to some students, it has many applications and helps students think about how their brains learn—by taking in new information through senses (seeing, hearing, tasting, smelling, and touching), processing the new input to think about how it might be useful, and storing it away in memory. The IPO model also describes how a computer processes information. The teacher reminds students of a computer programming phrase they may have heard: "Garbage in, garbage out." Applying this phrase to their independent study projects, the teacher cautions them that their finished product can only be as good as the information they gather, analyze, and apply to create it.

As the students proceed with their projects, the teacher checks in regularly. In the first phase, students submit a project proposal that spells out their mission statement and outlines the information they will need to gather. In the processing phase, when some students get bogged down or sidetracked, the teacher suggests that they return to their original plans for clarity. A few students submit revised plans based on new input they have gathered, which leads to another class discussion on what scientists do when they encounter unexpected results. As they enter the third phase of output, several students talk about switching gears from research and analysis to building their models or writing an outline for the presentation to accompany posters they have created to illustrate their findings.

When the projects have all been presented, the class participates in a debriefing session about what they learned—not just on their topics but on the process of independent study. The teacher is pleased to hear several students talk about how they proceeded through the input and processing phases. Everyone laughs when one student describes "taking out the trash" in referring to the need to set aside some irrelevant information he had found online so he could focus on the data that was most important. The teacher reminds students as they complete the discussion that the IPO model will be useful for projects in other classes and in high school and college—and even in their future jobs.

Lesson: Meeting the Brain's Chief Executive

Level: Middle and High School

This lesson might be appropriate for a science or health class on the human body and brain. It is also useful as an introduction to the concepts of brain plasticity and ways in which students can become functionally smarter by enhancing their cognitive assets and metacognitive approach to learning.

Step 1. Introduce this lesson on some basic facts about the human brain, how it changes in response to learning, and how metacognition can help us make the most of our malleable brains.

Step 2. Using a diagram of the four lobes in each hemisphere (see Figure 2.2), explain that the human brain is divided into two near-mirror hemispheres, on the left and right sides, and that each hemisphere is divided into four lobes, or sections. Using brain scans and other experiments and procedures, neuroscientists have discovered that each lobe has specialized functions:

- The *frontal lobes* are the center of foresight, planning, decision making, problem solving, and social skills and also

FIGURE 2.2

Diagram of the Brain

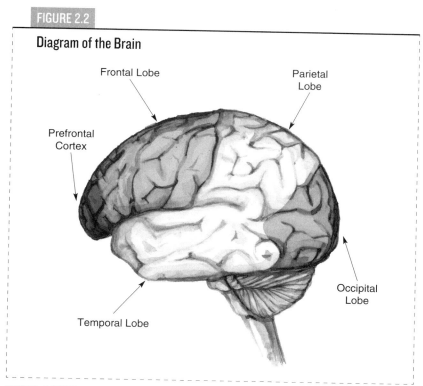

control body movements (Sylwester, 2005). The part of the frontal lobe known as the *prefrontal cortex,* which is directly behind the forehead, has been found to connect with every other functional unit of the brain (Swenson, 2006). Scientists believe the prefrontal cortex is responsible for coordinating most brain functions, and this section of the brain has also been shown to be most active in experiments where subjects are instructed to think about their thinking (Fleming, 2014). It is sometimes referred to as the "brain's CEO" or control center.

- The *temporal lobes* are the centers of processing most sensory input—what we hear, smell, and taste. These lobes help us process verbal communications.

- The *parietal lobes* are active when we are navigating, orienting the positions of our bodies and limbs, and processing tactile sensations.

- The *occipital lobes* are the brain's visual processing center.

For some aspects of processing thoughts and emotions, different lobes may work together. For example, the limbic system is a group of interconnected structures in the frontal and temporal lobes that regulate emotions and play a role in storing memories. The hippocampus, which is known as the gateway of memories, is part of the limbic system.

Step 3. Use the diagram to emphasize that specific areas of the brain gain volume when people engage in intensive learning and practice. For example, musicians who practice their instruments for hours every day and cab drivers who commit to memory the quickest routes through a city have larger hippocampi than other people. Another area of the brain that expands in response to learning is the prefrontal cortex; in fact, this section of the brain grows more than any other after birth (Swenson, 2006). Note that the prefrontal cortex has also been identified as the "headquarters" for metacognition and executive function. Learning, practicing, and improving thinking about our thinking and using cognitive assets like establishing our clear intent, focusing our selective attention, and monitoring our learning actually builds our brainpower and makes us functionally smarter.

Step 4. Explain that many people once thought of intelligence as fixed and unchangeable and that people's intellectual capacity was set at birth by genetics. Many thought that people were either smart or not smart and no amount of education and hard work to learn could change that, but we now know that learning changes the brain. This phenomenon is called "brain plasticity." When you learn something new, new connections form among the neurons in your brain. When you process that new information carefully, think about it in different ways, and apply it in other subjects and in life outside of school, the neuronal connections in your brain are strengthened. There's a saying among scientists that "practice makes cortex"—directing your thoughts and actions to learning new knowledge and skills will change your brain and make you functionally smarter. Explain that if you struggle with a particular subject, you can get better through determination and persistent hard work. Using metacognition along with learning and practicing cognitive assets can make the sometimes hard work of learning easier and more productive.

Step 5. Share an example of how metacognition can make the most of brain plasticity and over time make us expert learners. You might have a personal example or a story from your professional practice. Here's a common example that might resonate with students: Ella is excited about a history assignment to create a presentation on "great Americans most people have never heard of." She knows the perfect subject, Septima Clark, an educator and author who was active in the civil rights movement. Ella finds great information online and some photographs for her presentation. But then she gets sidetracked by other assignments, and she misses an opportunity to get training on PowerPoint techniques offered during her study period. She ends up rushed for time and frustrated because she had to spend too much time with what she thought would be simple editing and design work. When she sees other students' work, Ella sees that hers is not up to par. The other presentations are well designed and tell interesting stories. She knows that her presentation didn't do her subject justice, so she decides to learn from that experience. For the next project, Ella purposefully chooses to do another presentation, but this time she schedules all the tasks and sticks to the schedule. After participating in the PowerPoint training session, she finds the process of creating her presentation much easier, even fun. This time around, she is pleased with her presentation, and her grade is another sign that all her advance planning was time well spent. Throughout her years in high school and college, Ella finds that this metacognitive approach to planning pays off again and again. The planning process is much more automatic, and Ella has also become known as a "presentation pro," the person fellow students go to with questions about designing their school projects. Ella has made the most of her brain plasticity by steadily improving her planning and presentation skills.

Step 6. Conclude the lesson by facilitating a discussion with students on how thinking about their thinking might help them do school more successfully. Ask for examples of subjects where they used to struggle and how they got better at learning. Emphasize that using the "language of learning" like *metacognition* and *cognitive assets* reinforces how students are developing their skills over time and reflects brain plasticity in action.

Step 7. Finish with a memorable point that one definition of *meta-* is "higher." Metacognition is higher-order thinking that students can use in all their studies and in their lives outside school to help build their brainpower.

Metacognition Checkpoint

Encourage students to make the most of their brain plasticity by asking themselves questions like these:

- Are there subjects in school that are tough for me? Does that mean I'll never do well in those classes? How can I get better?

- What does the research on brain plasticity mean for me as a student?

- What can I learn and apply from past experiences in which I learned a new skill or overcame a difficult challenge?

Neural Plasticity, Metacognition, and Your Professional Practice

Findings that brain plasticity persists throughout the life span (Fotuhi, 2013) offer good news for teachers. In support of this neuroscientific evidence comes research on the development of expertise, which indicates that people who excel in a variety of fields, from academics to athletes and artists, are not endowed with natural gifts but instead are reaping the rewards of years of dedicated intensive practice and steady progress to improve their skills. What distinguishes top performers is their commitment to hard work, not innate talent. Ericsson, Prietula, and Cokely (2007) argue that the formula for becoming an expert in one's field is to put 10,000 hours of deliberate practice into developing relevant knowledge and skills.

A metacognitive approach to teaching and learning can help optimize your efforts to improve your professional practice throughout your career. One teacher who studied with us said she was inspired by learning that neural plasticity means "I can still learn important, life-changing things!" Another told us that explicit instruction on the use of metacognitive and cognitive strategies helped improve her students' learning and was "a game changer for me, too."

Emma Oberlechner, who teaches U.S. History to 8th graders in Westminster, Maryland, says she has benefited professionally and personally by becoming more metacognitive about her teaching:

> I've learned to think through my own thoughts before reacting—or overreacting. I think some teachers sometimes might think about a student, "This is useless! I'm done. I give up on this one." I used to feel that way. I hated feeling that way. Learning these strategies and the research base behind them helps me to understand these kids a little bit better. I can stop myself when I start to think that way and tell myself: I don't know the whole story of this student. (Personal communication, April 20, 2015)

Ms. Oberlechner says she applies metacognition and cognitive assets like understanding others' points of view (see Chapter 6) and systematic planning (see Chapter 4) in her personal life as well. Even a simple habit like categorizing her grocery list before she goes shopping helps to save time and reduce stress. "And I tend to think more before I speak, which is helpful in my personal relationships," she adds. "I am better able to process my thoughts and feelings and think, 'Why am I getting upset right now?' These are simple strategies, but it can make a difference when we think about the reasons why these strategies really work and how we can use them in other aspects of our lives."

3

Practical Optimism to Improve Motivation and Productivity

An optimistic approach to school, work, and personal pursuits enhances creative thinking and problem solving (Amabile & Kramer, 2011; Fredrickson, 2009). Optimistic learners are better able to deal with stressful situations and more likely to persist in the sometimes hard work required to progress academically, motivated by the belief that they can accomplish their learning goals. Researchers working to guide students to become more optimistic about their learning and more resilient in the face of challenges have found that "positive mood produces broader attention, more creative thinking, and more holistic thinking" (Seligman, 2011, p. 80).

Practical optimism is defined as an approach to learning and life that focuses on taking practical positive action to increase the probability of successful outcomes (Wilson & Conyers, 2011b). Note that this definition emphasizes the need for action in support of one's positive beliefs that success is possible. Practical optimism is not just about thinking happy thoughts and expecting good things to happen. Learning does not come easily for some students, and even those who seem to learn effortlessly may struggle with some lessons and learning goals. By applying practical optimism in tandem with other cognitive assets presented in this text, students learn that they can make steady progress toward their goals with hard work and determination.

A solid body of research on the power of practical optimism has grown from the discipline of positive psychology over the last two decades (Compton & Hoffman, 2013). Martin Seligman (1998), one of the pioneers of this field, reported on the differences between 4th graders who approached challenging learning tasks with an optimistic mindset and their peers who seemed more pessimistic about their ability to complete the tasks. The optimistic students persisted in their efforts, asked questions, and stayed with each task until completion. The other students were more easily frustrated and gave up when a task became difficult. Schulman suggests that a belief in one's ability to achieve one's goals is a vital third element of learning success, alongside ability and desire to succeed: "Someone with the talent of a Mozart can come to nothing in the absence of that belief. This is particularly true when the task at hand is challenging and requires persistence to overcome obstacles and setbacks" (1999, p. 31). The benefits of an optimistic outlook extend to physical health and more positive personal relationships as well (Rasmussen, Scheier, & Greenhouse, 2009; Seligman, 2011).

In the work setting, several studies connect an optimistic mindset to greater productivity and more effective interactions with colleagues. For example, a *Wall Street Journal* study reports that employees with a positive outlook are 33 percent more likely to assist their colleagues than their pessimistic peers, 36 percent more motivated, and 31 percent more likely to achieve their professional goals (Pryce-Jones, 2012). In their research with diverse project teams tackling tough assignments, Amabile and Kramer (2011) found that "people are more creative and productive when their inner work lives are positive—when they feel happy, are intrinsically motivated by the work itself, and have positive perceptions of their colleagues and the organization." Thus, teaching young students about the power of an optimistic outlook may contribute to positive outcomes in their future careers.

These findings are consistent with educational research showing that learning is enhanced in positive school environments "where students feel safe, secure, accepted, and encouraged to take intellectual risks" (Wilson & Conyers, 2011a, p. 105). How students respond emotionally to learning challenges is influenced by

1. Brain chemistry (neurotransmitters associated with positive and negative moods are produced in response to external stimuli);

2. Genetics (medical research has established that about half of people's "baseline" feelings of well-being—their tendency toward optimism or pessimism—is inherited);

3. Their thoughts (reflections on and cognitive responses to experiences); and

4. Their behaviors (actions and interactions with others).

Three of these four factors are within students' control; aside from their genetic makeup, they can take charge of their thoughts and behaviors and, in doing so, affect the production of neurochemicals in their brains to keep rolling in a positive feedback loop in which progress toward achieving their learning goals keeps students motivated to persist until they succeed.

Teacher Emma Oberlechner suggests that middle school is an especially important time for explicit instruction on how to apply a practically optimistic approach to learning. "Middle schoolers are at that in-between age, still trying to find themselves," says the Maryland 8th grade teacher. "They're starting to think of themselves as 'smart' or 'dumb.' So this is a good time to convey the message that it's more about how hard you work and how much you work that determines success in school. That message can really turn things around for these students."

The differences between an optimistic and pessimistic outlook are not just in one's expectations about positive versus negative outcomes. Pessimists are more likely to take setbacks personally and to view them as pervasive and permanent (Seligman, 2011). A pessimist might react to a negative outcome by thinking, "I've screwed up everything, and it's never going to get better." An optimist, however, might react like this: "Well, that's unfortunate, but I do see some ideas for improving this in the future."

Students need reminders that a poor score on one test does not mean they will never master the lesson content. They need to hear that setbacks offer learning opportunities and that they can improve their performance by steadily developing their knowledge and abilities. In research with athletes in training, connecting positive results to their abilities ("Your free throws really made the difference in the second half!") and negative results to a lack of effort ("Tough loss. Looks like we need more practice on defense.") seemed to contribute to improvements in their performance over time (Lickerman, 2013). A metacognitive approach to developing practical optimism encompasses both the belief that success is obtainable and the requirement to back up that belief with positive and sometimes persistent action.

Teaching with Practical Optimism in Mind

For teachers and students, developing and maintaining an optimistic outlook about learning entails staying focused on achieving positive outcomes and identifying and carrying through on the action steps needed to realize those outcomes. The I-4 model represents a process of self-reflection on four factors that may affect students' approach to learning: information, interpretation, impact, and influence (Wilson & Conyers, 2011b, p. 149). Teachers can share these steps with students as a strategy for maintaining a positive focus in their academic pursuits:

Step 1. Consider pertinent *information* regarding your learning. For example, you get a bad grade on a math test.

Step 2. Think about your *interpretation* of that information. You might think, "I knew it! I'm just terrible at math." Or you might think, "If I had studied harder, I could have earned a better grade."

Step 3. Be aware of the *impact* of your interpretations. You are likely disappointed about your grade, but are you feeling discouraged and ready to give up or determined to improve your performance?

Step 4. Come up with a plan to *influence* your grade. For example, you could do an extra credit assignment to review the concepts you struggled with previously and improve your understanding. You could develop and carry out a plan to improve your study habits before tests.

Step 5. Review the four factors of the I-4 model with a different set of circumstances, such as getting a good grade on a school project or getting an unexpected call-back for an interview for an after-school job. Remind students of four questions they can ask to be metacognitive about a positive approach in working toward achieving important goals:

- What information am I receiving?
- How am I interpreting that information?
- How does my interpretation impact how I feel and how I think?
- What can I do to positively influence the situation?

Introducing Practical Optimism

To help introduce the cognitive asset of practical optimism to students and develop it as a tool for learning, we suggest using the following ideas:

Explain that how students think about their learning can affect their chances for success. If they believe they can succeed through hard work and practice, they will be more likely to do so.

Emphasize that students can adopt a more positive mindset about their ability to achieve their goals. Note that people with a more positive outlook perform better in school and at work, have better relationships with family and friends, and enjoy better health.

Share the definition of *practical optimism,* and underscore that a positive outlook must be combined with action to achieve goals.

Emphasize that a can-do attitude and persistence in developing new knowledge and abilities contribute to positive outcomes. When students suffer setbacks or are behind on assignments, focus your encouragement on the need to keep trying and to think through learning strategies that might help improve their learning.

Inject some fun into your classroom. Playing games or reading aloud a funny story that supports lesson content makes learning engaging and memorable—and enhances a positive classroom environment.

Celebrate the power of incremental learning, or making steady gains by continuing to apply and take the next step in developing one's knowledge and skills. Amabile and Kramer (2011) refer to this effect as the *progress principle*; in their workplace research, they found that "of all the things that can boost emotions, motivations and perceptions during a workday, the single most important is making progress in meaningful work." In the same way, an optimistic approach to learning can support the same upward spiral of small successes that motivate students to keep trying and improving as they go.

Lesson: Brightside, the Optimistic Puppy*

Level: Lower Elementary

This read-aloud story about Brightside, appropriate for preK and early elementary grade children, illustrates the message that when you are optimistic about your ability to learn and succeed, you are more likely to achieve what you set out to do. Before sharing this story, introduce the key terms *optimism* and *succeed*.

> Brightside is a happy puppy. When it rains, the other puppies are sad. But Brightside says, "I love puddles!" When it is time to go inside after playtime, the other puppies are sad. But Brightside says, "I love cuddling up next to the fire!" When it is bath time, the other puppies are sad. But Brightside says, "I love bubbles!" His mama calls him "my little optimist." Brightside doesn't know what that means, but it makes him happy just to hear her say it!
>
> Brightside has many favorite things. His most favorite thing is playing with his boy Jack. The puppy loves to go for walks with Jack and learn new things. He learns how to shake his paw. He learns how to bark when Jack gives him a signal. He learns how to balance a treat on his nose. Brightside doesn't always learn new things on the first try, but he knows that if he keeps trying, he will succeed.
>
> One day, Jack decides to teach Brightside how to catch a ball. "Oh, boy!" Brightside thinks. "A new favorite thing!" Jack throws the ball. Brightside runs fast and far. He runs so fast and so far the ball falls behind

him. "Great!" Brightside thinks. "Now I know not to run so fast and so far." Jack throws the ball again. This time Brightside runs slower and not so far. The ball sails over his head. "Great!" Brightside thinks. "Now I know not to run too fast or too slow. If I watch the ball carefully, this time I'll catch it." Jack throws the ball one more time. Brightside watches the ball fly through the sky, and he runs toward it at just the right speed. Then he jumps up and catches it!

"Yay!" Jack calls. "I knew you could do it."

"Yay!" Brightside barks. "I knew I could do it, too! All I had to do was keep learning and trying! I love catching balls!"

Activity. Invite students to share an important task they have recently learned how to do. Did they make mistakes trying before they learned how to complete the task successfully? Consider modeling by telling students what you have recently learned.

*This story is adapted with permission from *Thinking for Reading Curriculum,* by Donna Wilson and Marcus Conyers, © 2005 BrainSMART, Inc. All rights reserved.

Lesson: Treasure Hunters and Trash Collectors

Level: Elementary

Begin the lesson by sharing this story with students:

It seems that in life there are two types of people. The first are treasure hunters. Every day they seek out what is useful and positive and focus on it, talk about it, think about it, and treasure it. Each of these moments is treasured like a bright, shining jewel that they store in their treasure chest forever.

And then there are the trash collectors who spend their lives looking for what is wrong, unfair, and not working—they focus their energy and their time and their thoughts on the trash. And every day they put that trash into a big old trash can.

Now every day, the treasure hunters proudly carry their treasure into the future, while every day the trash collectors drag their big, heavy, smelly trash can from one day to the next. The question is, when they get to the end of the year, what does each person have—a treasure chest full of useful, positive memories or a trash can full of things they didn't like?

The choice is yours.

You get to decide. (Wilson & Conyers, 2011a, p. 243)

Step 1. Explain that the next exercise the class is going to do will allow all students to begin filling their own personal treasure chests with the good things in their lives.

Step 2. Ask students to think of and write down five good things in their lives. If any students seem to struggle with this direction, provide some examples. They might list their favorite people, good books they have read, their favorite things to do, and activities or sports they enjoy.

Step 3. When students have finished their lists, direct them to stand up so they can move around the room. They should speak to five different students, sharing their list and listening as the other students share theirs.

Step 4. When students return to their desks, point out that thinking about the good things in their lives can help make a positive difference and maintain an optimistic outlook about their ability to achieve the goals they set for themselves in school and in life.

Step 5. Encourage students to continue adding to their list of people, events, and things that make them happy and give them reasons to be thankful. Whenever they need a boost, remind them to think of the good thoughts and memories they have stored in their treasure chests.

Extenders. This lesson may strike a chord with middle and high school students as well. Massachusetts teacher Theresa Dodge shares a story about 7th grade teachers at Greenfield Middle School who noticed a negative mindset pervading their classes and sought to set their students on a more positive path. Each teacher read the treasure hunters and trash collectors story to students as a way to illustrate the difference that focusing on the positive can make. The teachers also created a poster depicting a brightly shining treasure chest on one side and a reeking trash barrel on the other; around the treasure chest were positive words and phrases that could replace negative words. The teachers used the terms "treasure hunters" and "trash collectors" as reminders to students about the benefits of thinking positively about their school work and interactions with teachers and peers. Over time, the atmosphere on the 7th grade floor became more positive and supportive.

Lesson: Change Your Outlook, Change the Outcomes

Level: Middle School

Ms. Oberlechner, who teaches U.S. History to 8th graders at East Middle School in Westminster, Maryland, has developed a minilesson on practical optimism she delivers in a small discussion group format with learners "who are struggling with being optimistic about school and ultimately about life." The central message is that approaching learning with a positive outlook helps keep the focus on what students can do to improve their academic performance.

Step 1. Introduce the concept of practical optimism and the message that students are in control of their minds and that, by making a conscious effort to be optimistic, they can change many types of outcomes.

Step 2. Ask students how many believe that people are either born optimistic or pessimistic and there's not much that can be done to change that. Remind them of previous lessons using cognitive and metacognitive strategies to make learning easier. The same goes for changing your outlook: by consciously steering your thoughts away from negativity and complaints and toward positivity and what you can do to achieve your goals, you can take charge of your thoughts and feelings.

Step 3. Explain that researchers have found that optimistic people are more likely than pessimists to succeed in achieving their goals in school, at work, and in life. Optimists also have better relationships with family and friends and better health, too.

Step 4. Ask for examples of how a positive outlook might improve their approach to learning and other aspects of their lives, now and in the future. For example, one of Ms. Oberlechner's students wants to become a hairdresser, so they discussed how a positive attitude might make clients feel good about coming to her salon.

Step 5. Emphasize that an optimistic outlook can be contagious. If they exhibit a positive attitude about school, other students in their learning groups are more likely to do so as well—and that makes it easier and more fun for everyone to learn. Ms. Oberlechner shares a diagram she has adapted of a Newton's cradle with happy and sad face characters to represent the transformative effect of an optimistic outlook. When one happy face ball bumps into three sad face balls, one by one, the sad faces begin to smile.

Over the course of several weeks of introducing and reinforcing these messages, Ms. Oberlechner reports that she began to see changes in the attitudes of students in the first group participating in the lesson. "It's still a struggle, and some of the students are still failing. But their attitude has changed. They don't want to fail anymore. They know they could do better, and they're working harder," she says. "At least three of the students have improved their grades to *B*s and *C*s. Even the students who are still hovering between *D*s and *F*s have better, more positive attitudes. They are more willing to work hard and open up a little bit more to me."

Extender. The message that our emotional responses and attitudes influence others' outlooks is an important lesson to share with high school students in career-readiness classes. Consider sharing the research presented earlier in this chapter, and do a search for other articles on the effect of a positive outlook on success on the job. For example, it's worth noting that people who display an optimistic attitude during their initial job interviews are more likely to be called back for a second interview (Noomii, 2013).

Metacognition Checkpoint

Encourage students to be metacognitive about developing and maintaining a positive outlook in their learning by considering questions like these:

- How do I react to setbacks in school and in life? Do I get discouraged, or do I think about how I can learn from the experience and use it to improve in the future?
- How can I use the I-4 model and practical optimism to make steady progress in meeting my learning goals?
- What are some examples in my schooling and in life where believing that I could succeed made a positive difference?

Practical Optimism in Your Professional Practice

In the complex and stressful career of teaching, developing and maintaining a practically optimistic outlook can help you alleviate anxiety and rediscover joy in your work. Teachers who've learned about the benefit of practical optimism tell us it has had a transformative effect on their practice. "Because I am a more positive person and am working on being more energetic, the students are reaping the benefits of a teacher who is more tuned into them and helping them learn," one teacher said. Another reported that "The concept of positivity has made a huge impact on my teaching—taking control of my own life and helping students to see they can take control of their learning."

The following strategies can help you to develop and maintain a mindset of practical optimism and to model this outlook in a way that sets a positive tone in your classroom and interactions with students, colleagues, and parents:

• The default mode of thinking for many people is on worries and negativity (Killingsworth & Gilbert, 2010), but it is possible to purposefully steer your thinking in a more optimistic direction. Picture positive outcomes. Think about a person, place, or story that always lifts your mood.

• If you start to feel down about yourself or your abilities, focus on your positive qualities. Recall your signature strengths as a teacher and the things you love most about your profession. Give yourself a compliment, even something simple like, "I never give up. I stick with a challenge until I work through it."

• When you encounter an obstacle, take a step back to brainstorm a variety of solutions. Consider even seemingly absurd ideas; at the very least, they may make you smile, and at times they may lead to innovative, unexpected remedies. Some problems, though, are intractable; in those cases, the best approach may be to set the quandary aside and focus on other tasks and issues you can tackle.

• Contribute to a positive school learning environment by maintaining an optimistic spirit in conversations with colleagues. If negativity is the prevailing spirit in your breakroom, don't contribute.

• Share research on the power of positivity with parents, with the message that believing that their children can succeed academically and modeling that attitude can make a difference.

• Stay focused on the UPside—actions and thoughts that are *useful* and *positive* (Conyers & Wilson, 2015). Complaining and obsessing on problems and mistakes are neither.

4

Goal Setting and Planning for Learning

To achieve their learning goals, students must first identify what those goals are and how they plan to accomplish them. Teaching students to establish their own learning goals and to develop a plan to work steadily toward attaining those goals helps them to become self-directed learners and equips them with valuable and versatile skills for success in school and beyond. The process of learning to establish goals "has an extremely important role in the structuring of higher mental processes, which characterize human intelligence," according to Feuerstein, Feuerstein, and Falik (2010, p. 56).

Clear intent refers to identifying and sustaining a well-defined sense of what one hopes to accomplish. When students establish their clear intent in learning, they are applying a metacognitive approach to defining their goals and monitoring their progress so that they stay on task. Research shows that academic performance gains range from 16 to 41 percent in classrooms where students are explicitly taught how and why it is important to set learning goals (Marzano, 2007).

Setting specific and challenging goals furthers learning by providing students with benchmarks to measure their progress and to motivate themselves to exert the effort to accomplish their aims. "A major reason difficult goals are more effective is that they lead to a clearer notion of success and direct the student's attention to relevant behaviors or outcomes" (Hattie, 2009, p. 164). In one classroom study, researchers found that the performance of students pursuing the most challenging goals was 250 percent higher than outcomes for students with much easier goals (Wood & Locke, 1987).

Examples of setting and achieving personal goals—such as saving money to buy a bike or developing an athletic or artistic ability—serve as practical models for students to illustrate the importance of applying these skills to school assignments. When teachers help students connect to classroom goals in ways that have personal meaning for them, there is a much greater chance they will be motivated to engage in the sometimes hard work required in learning.

Hand in hand with establishing clear intent is the cognitive asset of *systematic planning,* defined as appropriate planning behavior organized in a way that leads to a well-expressed outcome. Learning to plan effectively enhances students' thinking and problem-solving abilities (Mayer, 2011; Mayer & Wittrock, 2009). Through explicit instruction on the importance of developing and adhering to a plan of action, teachers can guide students to develop their own plans for learning, to systematically search for pertinent resources, to apply their developing knowledge and skills, and to monitor their progress.

As we have noted previously, the prefrontal cortex has been identified as the seat of metacognition in the brain. This area relays input to another region in the basal forebrain (at the front and lower part of the brain), called the *nucleus accumbens.* The nucleus accumbens is known as the brain's "reward circuit," part of a pathway that stimulates the production of the neurotransmitter dopamine in response to rewarding experiences, such as celebrating success in achieving a learning goal. Dopamine is involved in many brain functions, including important aspects of learning such as motivation, memory, and attention, which may be enhanced by becoming more metacognitive about establishing learning goals and planning how to achieve them. To tap into those connections, this chapter discusses the advantages of giving students choices in their learning projects; of breaking challenging goals into smaller, more manageable action steps; and of providing explicit instruction on how to develop organizational and time management skills.

Teaching with Goal Setting and Planning in Mind

The following five-step process offers a practical framework for establishing clear intent and developing and implementing plans to achieve learning goals. This process is useful for both students and their teachers who want to work toward peak performance. Each step is accompanied by examples for students in elementary and high school.

Step 1. Establish your clear intent. Formulate a positive, motivating goal that is ambitious, yet achievable. Be as specific as possible in describing the positive outcome you are aiming to achieve. Envision the benefits the goal will bring.

> *Example 1:* I will finish my projects in class on time. That way, I can get to free time in the learning stations at the same time as everyone else, and I will get my first choice on the station where I want to play.

> *Example 2:* I will improve my study habits so that I consistently earn an *A* on my history exams. Achieving this goal will not only improve my overall grade in that class but will also help me do better in all my classes and on the SAT, which I have to take next year.

Step 2. Develop a detailed action plan for progressing in a positive direction. Focus on "when-then" planning to help make your action steps more concrete.

> *Example 1:* When the teacher tells us what to do for our projects, I will listen carefully the first time so I don't have to redo it. When I get distracted by what the other kids are doing, I will think extra hard about what I need to do to finish my project. When I talk to the other kids, I will only talk about the project we are doing so I don't get slowed down.

> *Example 2:* When I am in study hall, I will spend the first 10 minutes reviewing my notes from the history discussion that day, highlighting the most important information, and writing down any points that I need to go back and review. When I do my homework, I will study in my room with the TV and phone off so that there are no distractions. When I am studying for a test, I will join the after-school study group and use the recall strategies we learned in class.

Step 3. Focus on executing the action steps in your plan.

Example 1: When it is time to do our projects, I pay attention to the HEAR steps (see Chapter 5): I *halt* everything else I am doing, I *engage* with what the teacher tells us, I *anticipate* what my project will look like when I'm done, and I *replay* what she tells us to do while I'm working on my project. Sometimes, it's hard to keep paying attention, though, because it gets kind of loud with everyone talking, and my friends who sit next to me fool around sometimes.

Example 2: Our next history test is on Thursday, so I am going to the study group on Tuesday and

Wednesday. And when I study at home in the evening, I use memory pegs (see Chapter 5) to help remember the historical events that will probably be on the test in the right order, and I'm transferring my notes into a timeline diagram that I will be able to picture in my head. But I have a paper due this week in English, too, so that's cutting into my study time.

Step 4. Assess, monitor, and adjust your thoughts and actions as you execute your plan and after you complete an action step.

Example 1: I got to go to the learning stations with everyone else three times this week, so I got my first choice at the building station instead of having to wait until the other kids got done. And I'm doing better on my projects, too, because I'm not hurrying through them and trying to take shortcuts. My teacher thinks they look good, too!

Example 2: I got a *B* on the test, which is pretty good. I did better on the multiple choice part than in the past, so my study skills must be getting better. But my answers to the essay questions were kind of skimpy and not very well organized.

Step 5. Aim for steady gains in a positive direction and look for ways to improve the process.

Example 1: The one time I didn't get my project done on time was because I forgot a step. My teacher reminded me that she writes the step on the white board as she says them, so I can always look up there and make sure I'm doing all the steps.

Example 2: My friend did better on the essays than she did on the multiple-choice questions, so we made a plan to share test-taking tips and study together next time. Plus, the teacher put examples out on our class wiki of good essay responses from past years along with suggestions on planning how to write them, so that should be helpful.

As you can see from these examples, these steps form an iterative process. By regularly revisiting one's clear intent, it is easier to develop and implement a plan for learning, to evaluate progress, and to identify the need for revising the plan or adding additional steps.

Introducing Clear Intent and Systematic Planning

To help introduce the cognitive assets of clear intent and systematic planning to students, we suggest using the following ideas:

Emphasize the first step of achieving important goals. Clearly state those goals and then develop a plan to reach them. This process applies to learning in school and in life.

Define clear intent. Identify and sustain a well-defined sense of what one hopes to accomplish.

Achieve big goals using small steps. Throughout their years in school, in their personal lives, and in their future careers, your students will have many goals, some small and manageable and others large and intimidating. Explain that the best way to achieve big goals is to develop a series of smaller, more manageable steps so you can keep making progress.

Introduce the five-step process. Remind students the process is to set a clear intent, plan, execute, assess, and aim for steady progress.

Give students choices in learning projects and activities when possible. Allowing students to choose what they will research and study and how they will convey what they have learned enhances motivation and underscores that they are in charge of their learning.

Model clear intent and planning in your daily interactions with students. Begin lessons with explicit statements of goals and expectations. It may be useful to post a daily learning agenda on the board to help students get organized and focus on the subject of the day's lessons.

Consider beginning new units and projects by having students fill in a graphic organizer to identify the "what" they will be studying and "why" it is important. New Jersey middle school teacher Therese Reder guides her students to complete a graphic organizer on their topic of study that becomes a touchstone to keep them on track as they research and record information from diverse sources.

During check-ins on independent research projects and learning activities, remind students that developing a plan and schedule and sticking to it serves as a roadmap to success.

Lesson: Super Powers for Learning

Level: Lower Elementary

Developing a plan for solving problems and completing projects is one of the "super powers" of learning, according to a lesson created and delivered by library media specialist Kelly Rose to students in preK–2nd grade at the Out-of-Door Academy in Sarasota, Florida. Ms. Rose introduces a process for attaining learning goals in three steps—plan, do, and review—with the help of Super3, the library's superhero character she created inspired by *The Adventures of Super3: A Teacher's Guide to Information Literacy for Grades K–2* (Nelson & DuPuis, 2010). The character demonstrates the steps to solve problems and even "reads along" with Ms. Rose to see if storybook characters are good problem solvers.

In *Turkey Trouble* (Silvano, 2009), for example, the main character is worried about ending up as the main course as Thanksgiving approaches, so he plans to masquerade as other farm animals, but one disguise after another falls short. "He has to plan, do, review, do, review, do, review, and so on, until he finally finds a plan that works," Ms. Rose says. "The children realized that perseverance and creativity are extremely important when self-monitoring."

In explaining the steps to develop a learning plan, implement it, and review the results, Ms. Rose emphasizes that the need to go back and revise a plan, collect additional information, or try a different problem-solving strategy does not represent failure, but an opportunity to learn more about the subject. "By taking these steps, students learn a lot about themselves as individuals and are able to take control of the improvements they want to make themselves," she notes.

Applying this approach to a 2nd grade science research project, students working in small groups are assigned the task of researching the life cycle of a butterfly and then creating a project to share what they have learned with the class. The teacher reminds them that each group will likely need to work through at least two rounds of plan-do-review: the first to conduct their research and the second to plan and implement their project.

Step 1. Plan. Each group meets to assign research duties: conducting an online search, consulting the school's encyclopedia software, looking at books and files available in the classroom library, and going to the school library to search for books and resources.

Step 2. Do. Students conduct their research, share the information they have gathered, and make sure the sources are in agreement.

Step 3. Review. Students think about other questions they may need to answer before beginning their project. For example, how long does each stage last? Do butterflies lay their eggs on particular types of leaves? What do caterpillars eat? Some groups are thinking ahead to the next step of the project and decide that each student in their group should do additional research on a specific stage of the butterfly life cycle.

Step 4. Plan. After a final review of their information gathering, the groups plan how to present their project. Some choose to make a poster with labels, others plan to create a three-dimensional model, and still others decide that each student will create a costume representing a stage and present a short report.

Step 5. Do. Work on their projects proceeds over two class sessions, and some students work on their assignments at home as well. In a third session, the teacher suggests that each group "rehearse" their presentation, so that all students agree on how each of them will contribute. On the day of the presentations, the class is quite attentive to each group's project. The teacher notes that although each project covered the same basic information, each group added some unique facts to expand the knowledge of the whole class about butterflies.

Step 6. Review. Students complete simple rating forms on how they did individually and as a group planning, researching, and doing their projects and make suggestions about what they might do differently on their next project.

Lesson: Gathering and Organizing Data for a Research Report

Level: Middle School Social Studies

This lesson is appropriate as an introduction to planning and researching a report or as a refresher at the start of a school term. It focuses on an assignment to write a report on a famous historical figure, but the lesson could be adapted for use in any content course.

Step 1. The teacher begins by stating some commonly known "facts" from U.S. history: Columbus discovered America. George Washington was so honest that he confessed to his father about cutting down a cherry tree. Paul Revere was the lone, brave rider who rode through the countryside alerting colonists that "the British are coming!" Then she notes that these stories, though generally accepted as true, are either myths or do not represent the entire story. For example, the North American continent was inhabited long before Columbus arrived, and he wasn't even the first European to arrive; the Vikings arrived first. The story about Washington and the cherry tree is more of a fable than a fact. And

William Dawes was dispatched in the opposite direction from Revere to spread the word about the British, and others—as many as 40 riders—helped sound the alarm.

Step 2. The teacher introduces the assignment: Each student is to research and write a report about a person from history. The twist is that the report has to be surprising. A student might decide to research a famous story about a historical figure and report on whether it is true, false, or not the whole story. Or a student might research a little-known figure who played a big part in history.

Step 3. The teacher leads a discussion on how students might choose their research subject. One option students mention is researching "what they think they know about famous people" to see if it is true. Another is to research "myths about U.S. history," choose an interesting topic, and then track down the real story.

Step 4. The teacher notes that establishing clear intent to research a surprising story about a historical figure is the students' first step in planning the report. The second is to plan a systematic search for information from reliable sources. What constitutes a reliable source? The teacher asks for examples of where they might seek out accurate, objective information. The students mention online encyclopedias as well as encyclopedias in the school library, which also has shelves and shelves of books on U.S. history and historical figures. One student says she might go to the local historical museum to research little-known historical figures close to home.

Step 5. Though the class has discussed Wikipedia in the past, the teacher reminds students that this source cannot be considered reliable, though it may offer "leads" to other resources the students can explore. The teacher then begins a discussion about other online sites that may feature slanted or inaccurate views of history, such as sites championing a particular political point of view and online articles that do not include reliable references.

She then distributes a list of recommendations and questions for assessing the validity of online articles as academic sources.

Step 6. Verifying information with more than one reliable source is another way to separate fact from possible fiction, the teacher notes. For this assignment, students will be required to check and list at least two sources for the information included in their reports.

Step 7. In concluding the lesson, the teacher notes that this approach to systematic planning and research will come in handy in other classes this year and in high school and college. She asks students for examples of how finding reliable sources of information might be important on the job and in life. The students brainstorm a variety of situations: inventors conducting research on their creations, voters fact-checking political claims, families researching possible vacation destinations, and consumers researching a purchase or trying to find instructions to make a repair. The teacher applauds the students' long list of examples where systematic planning and research can help people make progress toward achieving their goals. This same approach will guide them to do a good job on other research reports, she reminds them.

Extenders. To introduce systematic planning and research at the elementary level, it might be useful to provide students with a short list of questions:

- What I want to learn: [guide students to write their research question]
- Where I can find the facts: [lead a discussion about sources of information]
- How I know these facts are reliable:
    - ☐ Found them in a trusted source (a nonfiction library book or encyclopedia).
    - ☐ Found them in more than one reliable source.
    - ☐ Learned them from an expert (like a scientist at a museum or a speaker to our class).
    - ☐ Other: _____

Lesson: Preparing for a Job or College Interview

Level: High School Speech or Career Class

Goal setting and planning are essential in preparation to apply for a job and perform well in a job or college interview. The need to set goals and to plan to effectively communicate in these important situations is reflected in the Common Core Career and College Readiness Speaking and Listening Standards for grades 11–12. The standards call for students to be able to "present information . . . conveying a clear and distinct perspective, such that listeners can follow the line of reasoning, alternative or opposing perspectives are addressed, and the organization, development, substance, and style are appropriate to purpose, audience, and a range of formal and informal tasks" (NGACBP/CCSSO, 2010a, p. 50). Teachers leading a lesson on developing and applying communication skills for students' future college or career searches can share these tips on preparing for a job interview.

Do your homework. You can discover a lot of information about prospective employers by visiting their website and Facebook pages, especially the news release sections. If their corporate history is available, you can gain insight into the major changes that have taken place over the years and how much those changes contributed to their success. Look for details about what products and services a company offers, what kinds of job openings are listed on its employment page (not just the job you're applying for), and what its customers say about the company. Pay special attention to clues about what skills and talents the organization expects of its employees (Smith, 2013).

Prepare for likely questions. The company will ask some questions specific to the position for which you are applying, but questions like these are common:

- "Tell me about yourself." Prepare a short answer (about one minute long) about your work and related experience (including school, activities, volunteer experience), and aspirations.

• "What interests you about this job?" Focus on what you can bring to the job, not what benefits you hope to gain (like salary, health insurance, or easy access from public transportation).

• "Why are you looking for a new job?" Don't look on this question as an invitation to complain about your current or former employer. If you were laid off or completed a limited-term position, state the reason simply and focus on the opportunities you hope to find in a new position.

• "What are your goals?" The goals you share should be consistent with and support the prospective employer's mission. This might also be a good time to mention goals to develop your on-the-job knowledge and skills so that you can be the best worker you can be and advance your career.

• "What are your strengths and weaknesses?" One way to respond to questions about weaknesses is to share an example of how you overcame a shortcoming by developing new skills.

• "What salary are you seeking?" Employers typically ask this question to ensure that job candidates would accept their standard pay range. If the company listed a pay range in its job ad, you could mention that wage as acceptable. If job research has turned up the average pay range for the job you are seeking, you can use that information in formulating a response that won't price you out of a job.

Employers sometimes ask unexpected, even silly, questions to give job prospects the chance to demonstrate their thought processes, creativity, and communications ability; to showcase their values and character; and to indicate how they would perform under pressure (Green, 2015). You may not be able to anticipate every question, but practice with interviews can help you become more comfortable with the process so you are more likely to respond in a forthright and engaging way.

Practice, practice, practice. Interview yourself or ask friends or family to serve as mock interviewers so you can become more familiar and comfortable with the process.

Know your career goals. Think short term and long term in deciding what skills and abilities you need to develop to land your dream job. What are you good at? What do you like doing? Would you be happy working outdoors? Do you enjoy interacting with people? Are you into technology?

Be positive. "It's all about your perspective, and in an interview being positive counts" (Smith, 2013).

Metacognition Checkpoint

Encourage students to be metacognitive about goal setting and planning in their learning by considering questions like these:

- What is my clear intent in this class? On this assignment?
- What do I want to achieve, and what steps do I need to take to do that?
- How will I know when I have achieved my goal?
- How does this goal fit within my bigger plan?
- Am I making positive progress, or do I need to revise my plan?
- If revisions are necessary, how can I best revise my plan?

Goal Setting and Planning in Your Professional Practice

Teaching is an incredibly complex profession, and it can be made even more so by myriad new programs, standards, and curricular requirements imposed at the school, district, and state level. Many mandates share the stated purpose of improving teaching and students' academic outcomes. In combination, they may seem to just make your job more complicated. It can be helpful to specify your professional goals within those standards and program mandates—to keep your eye on what drew you to teaching in the first place and to maintain your professional motivation and positive outlook.

Formulating Clear Intent

The five-step process set out in this chapter offers a practical framework to formulate clear intent for teaching a lesson or unit, to plan for its delivery, and to "assess in place" its effectiveness and any modifications to the lesson content and activities. Coauthor Marcus Conyers offers this example from a classroom activity he conducted for a lesson on fiction.

Clear intent. Goal 1 is to create an understanding of the structure of fiction in terms of characters, setting, plot, challenge, resolution, and moral of the story. Goal 2 is to create opportunities for all students to problem solve and to create solutions.

Plan. To use a strategy I developed called Story Scape. Here the teacher acts out a story, with input from students. Then students are asked to recall the elements of the story in terms of characters, setting, plot, challenge, resolution, and moral. A metacognitive aspect of planning is to make sure this strategy is an effective way to achieve my teaching goals.

Execution. I monitor student responses and involvement throughout the lesson to assess the following:

- Are my students demonstrating engagement?

- Are the quieter, shyer students contributing?

- Am I honoring students' backgrounds and experiences by encouraging them to share their ideas and perspectives?

- Am I keeping the process on track?

- Are students analyzing the problem and creating a solution that makes sense in the context of the story?

- Are students feeling a sense of success in the process?

- Am I facilitating opportunities for students to experience the creation of key elements of a story: (a) characters, (b) setting,

(c) plot, (d) challenge, (e) resolution of the challenge, and (f) the moral of the story?

- Are we all learning in this process?

Assess. After the lesson, I take a step back to assess how well the goals were met in terms of the criteria established in planning the lesson. I also look for evidence of a longer-term positive effect on students' ability to transfer their learning. The goals of the lesson were confirmed the next day when a reluctant learner came up to me and said, "Have you been talking to Disney with this story stuff? Because I was watching my cartoons last night, and they had all the stuff we talked about yesterday: character, plot, problem, and a way to solve it." I told him I was impressed with the brilliant connections he had made!

Aim for steady improvement. Following the lesson, I review students' responses and identify a few areas where I could make the key content even clearer for students.

- Expand the introduction to the elements of fiction and refer back to those elements more often in the discussion.

- Direct the students to write down the elements of fiction so they can refer to them during our discussion and when working on their own.

- After the initial lesson, assign the students to small groups to begin to create their own stories with some scaffolding from me.

The lesson. I share the story scape strategy. The students are mostly from low-income families, the children of migrant farm workers, with limited English proficiency and background knowledge. They are bright-eyed, brimming with potential, and a joy to work with, though they lack confidence in their ability to write a story. With the story scape strategy, I act out a story based on the creative input from all students. Usually the stories end up with my character in great peril. My goal is to make sure that even the shyest students contribute and that all experience the thrill of success fed by the release of dopamine in their brains over this positive, energizing experience.

We begin with the invitation to complete the opening line, "Once upon a time there was a man who was wearing . . . ?"

"An Elvis Presley outfit," the first contributor suggests.

"And he was looking for a . . . ?" I prompt.

"Guitar," pipes up a previously reluctant learner who is now at risk of not being the coolest kid in class, because his friend who made the first suggestion is now the center of attention.

"And then he heard a terrifying sound behind him, and he began to run because he was being chased by . . . ?"

"A giant frog!" exclaims another student.

"A giant *purple* frog!" supplies another.

As I act out the part of a man dressed as Elvis, looking for a guitar as he is pursued by a giant purple frog, I ask the students, "What happens next?"

"He trips over the guitar, and the frog is going to get him!" This suggestion is greeted by peals of delighted laughter.

"OK, now what creative way can he solve his problem?" I ask.

The room falls silent, as every brain strains for an innovative solution to this dilemma. Some students look pensive and others a bit anguished, and I can almost see them playing out various scenarios before their minds' eyes (which is itself a strategy that facilitates creative thinking).

In a quiet voice, a shy girl who has yet to speak says, "The Elvis man picks up the guitar and sings the giant purple frog a lullaby, so he goes to sleep."

Wow. I am stunned by how perfect her solution seemed, and so are her teacher and classmates. Our silence is broken by a great spontaneous round of applause. Then the excited students set out to write their version of the story, adding details about the characters, plot, plight, and resolution.

This story scape experience captures a great deal of what has fueled my passion for developing strategies to cultivate the cognitive skills that underpin creative writing so that every child is empowered to create his or her own story.

5

Selective Attention and Working Memory

Educational literature is full of discussions about the importance of gaining and holding students' attention during class time—and with good reason. Recent studies indicate that students' minds are more likely to wander in school and while studying than in any other daily endeavor; 76 percent of students in one study reported lapses in attention in academic settings (Szpunar, Moulton, & Schacter, 2013). This challenge is not new, but distractions both in the classroom and in students' after-school study environments are abundant. We will present some practical instructional strategies designed to enhance students' attention to classroom learning in this chapter, but at the center of teaching for metacognition is conveying the idea that students can take charge of their attention.

Selective attention is defined as the skill of identifying what is important in any given situation and attending to what is necessary with appropriate focus. The ability to focus on lesson content and to attend to learning tasks is a fundamental aspect of self-regulatory behavior that can be enhanced through deliberate practice. Attention serves as a baseline for higher-order thinking processes, including self-regulating thoughts and behavior, making meaning of new information, and employing memory strategies to enhance long-term recall (Miller, 2007). Explicit instruction on selective attention can help students learn to become better listeners, to take the initiative on learning tasks, and to set a realistic pace for making steady progress on their learning goals. As psychology professor Barry Schwartz contends,

> The key point for teachers and principals and parents to realize is that *maintaining attention is a skill.* It has to be trained, and it has to be practiced. If we cater to short attention spans by offering materials that can be managed with short attention spans, the skill will not develop. The "attention muscle" will not be exercised and strengthened. (2013, par. 5) [italics in original]

Developing selective attention can also help students enhance the cognitive asset of working memory. The term *working memory* refers to "the conscious processing of information" (Alloway & Alloway, 2013, p. 4) or, as Cowan defines it, "memory as it is used to plan and carry out behavior" (2008, p. 3). Cowan offers these examples of working memory in action:

> One relies on working memory to retain the partial results while solving an arithmetic problem without paper, to combine the premises in a lengthy rhetorical argument, or to bake a cake without making the unfortunate mistake of adding the same ingredient twice. (2008, p. 3)

Alloway and Alloway underscore the connection between attention and working memory: The latter involves "giving attention to [information], shining a mental spotlight on it, concentrating on it, or making decisions about it. You are also intentionally ignoring everything else" (2013, p. 4). *Working memory capacity* has been defined as "the capacity to selectively maintain and manipulate goal-relevant information without getting distracted by irrelevant information over short intervals" (Jha, Stanley, Kiyonaga, Wong, & Gelfand, 2010, p. 55). Studies indicate that students can learn to direct their attention to make the most of their working memory and can improve their academic performance by enhancing their ability to identify, focus on, and process the most important information among all inputs.

Honing working memory helps students think faster, weigh the pros and cons to make better decisions, adapt to new situations, and maintain motivation to achieve long-term learning goals. A graduate of the brain-based teaching program at Nova Southeastern University linked the cognitive assets of selective attention and working memory and credited them as among the most important thinking skills to teach: "Paying attention when it matters. I think that it affects all aspects of learning because if you can pay attention, you are more apt to remember what is most important. If students can listen, pay attention, and collaborate with others, they will be most likely to succeed." And as students develop their selective attention and working memory, the need for teachers to manage behavioral issues may decline as self-directed learners spend more time on task.

Emerging research from educational neuroscience suggests that working memory is a better predictor of school achievement than intelligence quotient—and that schools and teachers can help students enhance their working memory through explicit instruction and in the effective organization of classrooms and the daily learning schedule (Alloway & Alloway, 2013). Applying this research can have a significant effect on academic progress, especially for students with learning challenges. A vital message for students is that consciously working to develop their selective attention and working memory will help them to do better in school, in their future jobs, and throughout their lives. The following applications of recent research on these cognitive assets can help all students make the most of their "think space" across core subjects.

Teaching with Selective Attention and Working Memory in Mind

"Because learning is the goal of instruction and studying—and because learning depends on attention—mind wandering presents a particular challenge to education" (Szpunar et al., 2013, concluding comments, par. 2). The following teaching strategies can help engage students' selective attention and guide learning without overtaxing their working memory.

Apply the CRAVE Formula

The five elements of the CRAVE formula—curiosity, relevance, asking questions, variety, and emotions—provide a versatile toolkit of strategies you can use in planning and presenting lessons and learning activities to make the most of selective attention and working memory with students at all grade levels (Wilson & Conyers, 2011a).

Strategy 1. Build **curiosity** for learning. Advertisers and online content providers are experts at grabbing your attention and compelling you to click on intriguing headlines and mysterious images (e.g., "Man Has Bizarre Collection," "Path to Stardom Had Unlikely Start," "The Rest of This Photo Is *Really* Strange"). You can apply these tactics in introducing lessons with interesting facts ("Today we're going to discover why we should *love* spiders") and "teasers" ("Algebra can make you a better shopper, and in the next couple weeks we're going to find out how"). Riddles are another way to get a lesson off to a positive, engaging start, to focus students' attention on the language at the heart of a lesson, and to demonstrate that learning can be fun:

- For math class: What is a math teacher's favorite dessert? (Pi)

- In a geometry review: What figure is like a lost parrot? (A polygon)

- In a grammar lesson: What do you call Santa's helpers? (Subordinate Clauses)

- In U.S. geography: What did Delaware? (Her New Jersey)

- In a lesson about how animals protect themselves: Why can't a leopard hide? (Because he's always spotted)

- In a lesson about astronomy: When is the moon the heaviest? (When it's full)

Strategy 2. Make lessons **relevant**. Connecting the curriculum to students' lives and engaging their prior knowledge helps to build interest in learning and emphasize what students already know (or think they know) about a topic so they can expand on that knowledge base. For example, begin a unit on state history by exploring what life was like for children when the state was first being settled or achieved statehood in comparison with what life is like for children who live in the state today. Or, guide students to understand the practical benefits of honing their math skills by calculating and comparing the savings in special offers in store flyers and coupons.

Strategy 3. Ask questions that gauge students' understanding, pique curiosity, or encourage them to transfer new knowledge to other areas to aid in engaging their attention throughout a lesson. In a study that has implications for lecture-heavy high school classes, researchers found that inserting low-stakes quizzes and poll questions that can be answered with clickers or a show of hands help keep students engaged (Bunce, Flens, & Neiles, 2010).

Strategy 4. Remember that **variety** is the spice of attention. Change how you deliver new lesson content—use lecture, class and small group discussions, hands-on activities, creation of visual representations, and participation in learning games to hold student interest and reinforce the information. Interspersing teacher talk with learning activities also engages more of students' senses, supplementing auditory input with visual and tactile cues.

Strategy 5. Evoke **emotions** to hold attention. For example, history can be dry and boring when instruction centers on rote memorization of dates and events, or emotionally stirring and rousing when the focus is on the powerful forces and events that compel certain behaviors and change the course of people's lives. Stories that bring people and events to life are provocative; disparate facts are not. The prevalent emotions in a classroom learning environment also influence students' attention to learning: they have a more difficult time focusing on lesson content, studying, and learning tasks when they are tired, anxious, or bored (Szpunar et al., 2013). In comparison, a positive learning environment in which students feel safe, secure, accepted, and encouraged to take intellectual risks (see Chapter 3) is conducive to maintaining their attention.

Avoid Instructions Overload

According to Alloway and Alloway, "understanding instructions is one of the most demanding tasks for a student's working memory. They have to keep the set of instructions in mind as well as execute each one in the proper sequence. Too many instructions can easily overwhelm a student or a whole class" (2013, p. 104). To avoid confusing or frustrating students, limit the instructions based on the age of students. For example, in a kindergarten or 1st grade class, limit instructions to two at a time. Older elementary-age students should be able to follow a sequence of three instructions; middle school students, four instructions; and juniors and seniors in high school, six instructions. For all grade levels, it may be helpful to share important instructions in written form so students can refer to them as they complete assignments.

Introducing Selective Attention and Working Memory

To introduce the cognitive assets of selective attention and working memory to students, we suggest using the following ideas:

Make the point that we all can learn to direct attention to what is most important at the time and to improve memory skills.

Define the terms *selective attention* and *working memory.*

Ask for examples of how improving selective attention and working memory might be beneficial inside and outside the classroom.

Emphasize that thinking skills can be used in all subjects and outside school. Ask how their parents might use these skills at work and how they will come in handy in college and throughout their careers.

Think aloud when you use selective attention and working memory in your teaching, and look for opportunities to recognize students for using these cognitive assets.

Remind students to be metacognitive about their selective attention and working memory by monitoring whether they are focusing appropriately on the learning task.

Lesson: Calm Cool, the Listening Rabbit*

Level: PreK and Lower Elementary

Introduce the central message of the story. Tell students that by becoming a better listener like Calm Cool, they can learn a lot!

Calm Cool is the best listener in Happy Warren School. But this was not always so. Do you know why Calm Cool became such a good listener? Because he LOVES carrots. Not all rabbits like carrots, but Calm Cool LOVES them. He loves carrots because they are bright orange. He loves carrots because they are crunchy. He loves carrots because they are so DELICIOUS. What Calm Cool does not love is how hard it is to find the best carrots in the school garden.

One day, Calm Cool was sitting with his friend Naughty Paws as their teacher, Ms. Hare, was teaching everyone about taking care of the garden. All the rabbits were listening carefully except for Calm Cool and Naughty Paws. Instead of listening, they were giggling and playing silly rabbit games. So they did not hear

Ms. Hare when she whispered a secret: "The best carrots are in the middle of the garden, right behind the big oak tree." When the school bell rang for play and snack time, all the other rabbits ran to the middle of the garden. Calm Cool and Naughty Paws did not run to the garden. They ran to the fence. They played hopscotch. They played shadow games with their big bunny ears. When they finally went to the garden to get a snack, all the best carrots were gone.

"Why didn't anyone tell us there were such yummy carrots in the garden?" Calm Cool wailed as he watched his friends munching on delicious, crunchy, orange carrots. "Ms. Hare did tell us, silly," said Digger Dan before taking another big bite of his carrot. "You just weren't listening."

The next day, Calm Cool decided he would be the best listening rabbit he could be. He kept his eyes on Ms. Hare, not on Naughty Paws. He pointed his long bunny ears right at his teacher, even though all the rabbits around him were busy boasting about the yummy carrots they found yesterday. So when Ms. Hare leaned forward to share another secret, Calm Cool was the only one listening. Ms. Hare whispered, "Today the best carrots in the garden are behind the rose bush."

When the bell rang, Calm Cool was the first one through the door. He ran to the rose bush in the garden and found the brightest, crunchiest, most delicious carrot he had ever seen. Calm Cool thought, "Life is really good when you learn to be calm and cool so you can listen carefully!" And that is how Calm Cool became the best listener in Happy Warren School.

Activity. Explain that people can become better listeners through practice, the same way that they develop other skills, such as learning to read, learning to add and subtract, and learning to play sports. Then play a listening relay game similar to Telephone:

Divide students into groups of five or six, and direct them to sit or stand in a circle. Ask one child from each group to gather round you, tell them a secret sentence quietly and quickly, and send them back to their groups. That child will whisper the sentence to the child next to him or her—quickly and only once—and that child will pass it along to the next child, and so on. Emphasize that the goal is to pass the message on as quickly as possible. When the last child has heard the secret sentence, he or she says it out loud and each group will hear how much the message has changed.

After the first round, lead a discussion about how and why the secret sentence may have changed from the first student to the final student in each group. Maybe the children had a hard time hearing one another, or maybe they forgot one of the words before they could pass the sentence on. Talk about what students can do to improve their listening and passing along the message this time: They can listen more carefully. They can ask the student sharing the message to repeat it. They can say the message back to make sure they have it right before passing it along.

Now ask a different student from each group to come up for a new message. Remind the whole class that they should do their listening relay more slowly and carefully this time. Share the sentence more slowly and ask the children to repeat it before going back to their groups. Observe whether students are sharing and listening with more care. When the second relay is completed, have a follow-up discussion. Did the secret message make it through better this time? If so, why? And how might children use these more careful listening skills in class and at home?

*This story is adapted with permission from *Thinking for Reading Curriculum*, by Donna Wilson and Marcus Conyers, ©2005. BrainSMART, Inc. All rights reserved.

Lesson: Honing Selective Attention

Level: Upper Elementary

Like other aspects of learning and communicating, listening is a skill that can be learned and improved. The Common Core State

Standards for Language Arts recognize the need for students to learn to listen well, within the context of the acquisition of a host of verbal and social skills:

> Students must learn to work together, express and listen carefully to ideas, integrate information from oral, visual, quantitative, and media sources, evaluate what they hear, use media and visual displays strategically to help achieve communicative purposes, and adapt speech to context and task. (NGACBP & CCSSO, 2010a, p. 8)

A common obstacle to effective listening is noise—not just the sounds of a busy classroom (e.g., students talking, papers rustling, classes moving down the hallway), but also "interior noise" within students' minds—thoughts and daydreams that may distract them from what the speaker is saying. The HEAR strategy—halt, engage, anticipate, and replay—is designed to help students recognize and proactively block noise from both internal and external sources as they devote their attention to listening (Wilson & Conyers, 2011a). You can explain four concrete steps students can follow to be sure they are focused on listening:

Halt. Stop whatever else you are doing, end your internal dialogue on other thoughts, and free your mind to pay attention to the person speaking.

Engage. Focus on the speaker. We suggest a physical component, such as turning your head slightly so that your right ear is toward the speaker as a reminder to be engaged solely in listening.

Anticipate. By looking forward to what the speaker has to say, you are acknowledging that you will likely learn something new and interesting, which will enhance your attention.

Replay. Think about what the speaker is saying. Analyze and paraphrase it in your mind or in discussion with the speaker and other classmates. Replaying the information will aid in understanding and remembering what you have learned.

Initially, you may need to lead several demonstrations of using the HEAR strategy and remind students when it is time to HEAR, but over time listening should become more automatic. As Michigan teacher Aaron Rohde says, "Just saying that one is going to be a better listener is not enough to make it happen. One must work hard to improve such an essential skill." In fact, when Mr. Rohde introduces this strategy to 3rd and 4th graders, he wears a hardhat to emphasize that learning how to listen well is hard work. But he also tells his students, "Being a 'listening genius' will be beneficial in all areas of life—in school, in personal relationships, and in professional work situations."

Extender. The HEAR strategy can also be shared with middle and high school students in a speech or communications class in the context of debunking the "myth of multitasking." Many students are comfortable in a world awash with media: they may study at night with the TV on while surfing the web and texting their friends. However, experiments by neuroscientists show that the human brain is only capable of focusing on one thought or action at a time. The brain can shift from task to task very quickly, but it can't attend to two tasks simultaneously. That's why it's harder for students to retain what they are studying if their minds are shifting among a textbook, a TV show, a website, and messages from friends. It's also why the HEAR strategy is an effective approach to improve their selective attention to speakers in a classroom setting.

Lesson: Memory Pegs

Level: Upper Elementary

Specific strategies to increase recall can bulk up working memory capacity. By learning different ways to encode information, students develop their selective attention because they are more focused on thinking about their thinking and less likely to become distracted or frustrated. We have found that a strategy to enhance recall employing association, which we call *memory pegs* (Wilson & Conyers, 2011a), is a highly motivating activity that leads to positive discussion and reinforces students' beliefs that they can improve their learning.

Use these steps to introduce memory pegs to students.

Step 1. Ask students to stand in two rows and listen to a list of 10 words related to a lesson and to try to remember them all. In a health lesson, for example, the list might include nutritious foods such as blueberries, nuts, salmon, broccoli, bananas, frozen yogurt, olive oil, brown bread, spinach, and tomatoes.

Step 2. Ask students to turn to the person next to them and recite the list of words in order.

Step 3. Ask who remembers all 10 in order, 9 in order, 8 in order, 7 in order, and so on, and keep a tally of how many students remember each number.

Step 4. Ask students if they would like to learn a way to easily remember all 10 items on the list—and apply this strategy to other facts they need to remember.

Step 5. Guide students to mirror you as you tap "pegs" on your body: (1) head, (2) shoulders, (3) heart, (4) belly, (5) hips, (6) backside, (7) thighs, (8) knees, (9) shins, and (10) toes.

Step 6. Tap each of these pegs again, this time associating a word on the list with each:

1. Head–blueberries
2. Shoulders–nuts
3. Heart–salmon
4. Belly–broccoli
5. Hips–bananas
6. Backside–frozen yogurt
7. Thighs–olive oil
8. Knees–brown bread
9. Shins–spinach
10. Toes–tomatoes

Step 7. Direct students to recall the list in order as they tap their memory pegs. Compare how many students remembered fewer, the same number, or more of the words this time.

Step 8. Lead a discussion about other situations where the memory pegs strategy might be handy.

Extender. This strategy can be applied across content lessons and grades. In language arts, for example, students can use memory pegs to remember figures of speech to improve their writing. In science, they can improve their recall of the names of the planets or of elements on the periodic table. Emma Oberlechner teaches her 8th graders how using memory pegs can help them recall both the major battles of the Civil War and the chronology of those events. Memory pegs is also a popular strategy in our teacher workshops and offers an easy application to incorporate into your personal and professional toolbox of cognitive strategies. As just one example, memory pegs can help you recall the components of a lesson—and demonstrate this strategy in action for students!

Lesson: WIN Students' Selective Attention

Level: Middle School Health/Math

In teaching students that they can take charge of their selective attention, a useful mnemonic is WIN: what's important now? Students can use this simple, versatile checklist to stay focused on WIN:

- What is my clear intent (see Chapter 4) in this situation?
- What do I need to attend to so I stay focused on achieving my clear intent?
- What's most important right now in achieving my clear intent?
- What might I need to ignore to stay focused on what's important now?

Students can apply the WIN question in the classroom, in their studies, and in other aspects of their lives, such as making healthy food choices. For example, when choosing an after-school snack, it's important to select a food that is low in fat and sugar and rich in nutrients that will fuel their body and brains for after-school activities.

Applying this strategy to a health or math unit on junk food advertising, explain that advertisers apply their version of the WIN question in timing TV ads that entice viewers to order pizza and party foods. Direct students to analyze the food ads when they watch TV with their families. How many ads do they see for healthy food choices? Unhealthy? What is the timing of those ads? (Pizza ads, for example, often run in the late evening and on the weekend during sports broadcasts.) What serving portions are depicted in the ads? Some ads may promote foods as healthy choices but how healthy are they really? Assign students to do some research to estimate the caloric intake of the foods and portions depicted in the ads and to calculate what percentage of recommended daily calories are represented in them.

Their findings can inform a classroom discussion on the difference between the aim of junk food ads and the aim of people intending to maintain healthy eating habits. For example, students comparing the calories of different snacks might find that munching on four carrot sticks and four celery sticks translates to fewer than 20 fat-free calories, while a single slice of pizza may contain 250–400 calories, depending on the size of the slice and types of toppings.

Lesson: Explain It to Your Brain

Level: High School Independent Study

Who is the most attentive, on-task person in most classrooms? The teacher! As you know from personal experience, teaching others requires your full engagement and understanding of the lesson content. That's why peer teaching strategies are so effective—because students' understanding of a topic increases when they teach it to others. Another permutation of the "learning through teaching" dynamic is to share study strategies with students that encourage them to become their own teachers. Deploying these teaching tools while studying on their own can help students stay focused and reinforce their understanding as they explain it to their brains.

BrainWeb. Creating graphic organizers or depictions of key lesson concepts can help develop deeper meaning and enhance retention (Wilson & Conyers, 2011a, p. 251). Begin with a large outline of a brain. On the left side within the brain frame, draw pictures or symbols that represent important aspects of the lesson you are studying. On the right side, make notes to explain and expand on the graphical representations. Then draw arrows between the two sides to connect the graphics to your notes.

Summarize. Reducing a short story or a long passage in a textbook to a summary that captures the most salient and important points is a useful way to check your understanding and improve recall. Here's a fun and memorable way to summarize: identify the most important information you're studying and write it as a 140-character tweet as if posting on Twitter!

Question and answer. In class, teachers ask questions so that students can develop and demonstrate their understanding as they formulate an answer. You can do the same—ask questions—when studying on your own.

- In reading a fiction assignment for the first time, ask yourself, *what's going to happen next?* If your prediction is accurate, think about the clues in the story that pointed you in that direction. If not, go back and find the clues you might have missed the first time, or think about what motivated the characters to act differently than you expected.

- In working on math problems, ask yourself, *how can I double-check this answer?* There are often several ways to solve a problem. Using a different approach offers a way to check your work and expands your understanding of math principles.

- In a variety of subjects, ask yourself, *how are these elements alike and different?* Classifying and comparing are useful ways to investigate people and things. If Abraham Lincoln were alive today, which political party might he support? How are spiders different from bugs? Which breakfast foods are most nutritious? If you're studying transportation in geography, consider the following: For people living in cities, what's the fastest way to get to work? The cheapest? The most environmentally friendly?

Identify and use cues appropriately. A cue is information you can use to make a lesson more meaningful, to complete an assignment, or to solve a problem. Paying attention to both explicit and less obvious cues is an effective way to keep your brain tuned in to the most important information. Here are examples.

• When writers want to help their readers make interesting connections or see the world in a different way, they use literary devices (or cues!) such as metaphors, similes, and symbols. As you are reading a poem or story, look for these cues and think about the deeper meaning.

• Textbooks provide a variety of cues to focus attention on the most important content to study and review: key terms, subtitles, informational graphics, summaries, and review questions. A useful study strategy is to begin by skimming a textbook reading assignment with special attention to these cues. Then when you are done reading, revisit these cues to double-check your understanding.

• When conducting online research, look for cues that the information presented is accurate and impartial. For example, if you are researching nutritious meals, a website sponsored by a food manufacturer might not be an objective source.

• A common misstep in taking a test is to skip reading the instructions based on the assumption that you know what you are supposed to do. *Always* take the time to review the instructions and identify the cues about how you should be focusing your attention to successfully complete the test.

• Errors in solving math problems frequently hinge on conducting the wrong operation. If you're not paying attention to the signs in an equation, you may add when you're supposed to be multiplying or subtract when you should be dividing. When you're working on math problems on your own, translating these cues into words—as in "I need to divide 5,280 by 4"—can help make this step a habit.

Metacognition Checkpoint

Encourage students to be metacognitive about their selective attention and working memory by teaching them to ask themselves questions like these:

- What distractions do I need to recognize and avoid in directing my selective attention on learning?
- How did focusing my attention on the textbook make it easier to remember what I was studying?
- How could I use memory pegs in studying for an exam?

Becoming More Mindful in Your Professional Practice

The school day is full of distractions for students—and teachers. As we have noted previously, teaching is a complex and stressful profession, and these pressures can make it difficult to stay focused on your students' learning needs and to optimize your working memory capacity while juggling the many tasks of teaching. Over time, mindfulness training may help you develop the skills of regulating your attention and maintaining a positive attitude when interacting with students, colleagues, parents, and others (Jha et al., 2010). *Mindfulness* refers to a conscious state of awareness of your current thoughts, actions, and surroundings. The ability to keep your thoughts on the present moment, instead of allowing your mind to wander and worry, has been shown to improve selective attention, enhance positive outlook and feelings of well-being, and increase working memory capacity.

Mindfulness Practice

A simple beginning strategy for becoming more mindful is the exercise of concentrating on your breathing (this strategy could be shared with middle and high school students as well):

Step 1. Set aside 5 to 10 minutes in a quiet room where you won't be interrupted. Sit in a comfortable chair with your feet on the floor or on a cushion on the floor. Keep your back straight but relaxed. Rest your hands on your knees or in your lap.

Step 2. Consciously shift thinking from your typical mode of doing, planning, and worrying to simply being. Focus on your breathing. You don't need to change the way you are breathing in any way. Just be aware of the act of breathing in and out. Notice how your body feels and moves as you take air in and then exhale.

Step 3. When your mind wanders (and it likely will, unless you've been practicing mindfulness for a while), bring your attention back to your breathing and focus your consciousness on the duration from each breath in and out. Don't judge yourself for getting distracted. It will be easier to be mindful and in the moment the more you practice.

Step 4. As you continue to attend to the act of breathing, observe that you are feeling more relaxed and aware only of the state of being. When your thoughts drift away to other subjects—like something that happened at school or your plans for later in the day—steer them back to thinking about only the act of breathing and how it feels.

At the end of the time you have allotted for this exercise, you should feel refreshed and at ease. As with other endeavors, learning to be mindful gets easier and more effective with practice. Over time, you should be able to apply this strategy to clear your mind and refocus your attention on teaching or your personal pursuits outside the classroom.

6

Strategies for Self-Monitoring and Learning with Peers

Purposefully monitoring one's learning is at the heart of meta-cognition. To complete learning tasks, students need to learn how to self-monitor to ensure they are on track to finish successfully. They must know when and how to use metacognitive strategies, to assess the effectiveness of their use of these strategies, and to adjust. This chapter introduces cognitive assets that support successful completion of learning tasks, including monitoring progress, evaluating understanding of new material, and knowing when to use fix-up strategies.

Self-monitoring refers to the ability to track one's thoughts and actions in learning. Students who are adept at this meta-cognitive skill regularly ask themselves, "How well do I understand this lesson? How can I evaluate my understanding, and what more do I need to learn? How does this new knowledge fit with what I already know? And which cognitive assets can help me improve my learning?" For example, the Common Core State Standards emphasize the need for students to self-monitor for understanding as they read and for clarity and word usage as they write. The Language Arts Standards for 8th graders specify that students should be able to "demonstrate understanding of figurative language, word relationships, and nuances in word meaning," including figures of speech, relationships between words that affect their meaning, and the gradation of meanings that set synonyms apart from each other (NGACBP/CCSSO, 2010a, p. 53).

A key asset in self-monitoring is *cognitive flexibility,* the capacity to objectively consider two or more concepts simultaneously and to recognize when it may be useful to adjust one's thinking and actions based on new information. Students can be guided to develop this component of executive functioning so they can think through diverse or conflicting ideas, assess complex situations, and weigh the pros and cons of multiple solutions and alternatives. This cognitive asset is helpful in a variety of learning challenges, from solving "brain puzzles," where creative problem solving comes in handy, to taking high-stakes tests, where some problems may be specifically designed to require out of the box thinking. Developing cognitive flexibility can benefit everyone, whether in school or in the workplace. As adults, the ability to innovate and to understand the diverse perspectives of coworkers and customers will be highly valued.

Another element of self-monitoring is to evaluate one's effectiveness in learning with others. Teamwork and collaboration skills are prized 21st century competencies, and the Common Core State Standards for Language Arts identify "understanding other perspectives and cultures" as an important aspect of career and college readiness:

> Students appreciate that the twenty-first-century classroom and workplace are settings in which people from often widely divergent cultures and who represent diverse experiences and perspectives must learn and work together. Students actively seek to understand other perspectives and cultures through reading

and listening, and they are able to communicate effectively with people of varied backgrounds. They evaluate other points of view critically and constructively. Through reading great classic and contemporary works of literature representative of a variety of periods, cultures, and worldviews, students can vicariously inhabit worlds and have experiences much different than their own. (NGACBP/CCSSO, 2010a, p. 7)

In one specific example, the Speaking and Listening Standards for Grades 6–12 call for 8th graders to "pose questions that connect the ideas of several speakers and respond to others' questions and comments with relevant evidence, observations, and ideas" and to "acknowledge new information expressed by others and, when warranted, qualify or justify their own views in light of the evidence presented" (p. 49). This standard brings together the abilities of understanding other points of view and cognitive flexibility to optimize learning with peers. Developing empathy and the ability to understand other peoples' points of view is "an essential, active skill . . . foundational to embracing differences, building relationships, gaining a global perspective, conducting richer and deeper analysis, and communicating more effectively" (Tavangar, 2014). This skill is a vital cognitive asset that can be developed through practice.

Jess Young, who now teaches history to 7th to 10th graders who are learning English as a second language at the New American Academy, St. Louis Public Schools, has seen the positive effect of explicit instruction on empathy and understanding others' perspectives in helping students learn from each other more productively. In her former position, Ms. Young taught 8th grade math and social studies in a diverse Georgia school serving children from Caucasian, African American, Hispanic American, and Asian American backgrounds. Initially, discussions about racially charged subjects, such as the history of slavery in the South and economic inequality in the United States, became quite heated. "Students talked and yelled over each other and wouldn't listen," she recalls. "They had a hard time hearing other students' perspectives."

Then Ms. Young introduced the cognitive assets of understanding others' points of view and participating in civil debate. Students took the Empathy Quiz available online (Greater Good Science Center, n.d.) and received recommendations on enhancing empathy by becoming better listeners, looking for what they have in common with others, and paying attention to other people's facial expressions as a way to gauge their emotions. Their teacher emphasized the importance of being more empathetic in their interactions with fellow students and other people in their lives. Over time, hostility over sensitive subjects dissipated, and classroom discussions became more productive and positive.

Developing empathy can help students become more accepting of others who are different from them, Ms. Young suggests. She cites the example of one student with Asperger's syndrome and attention deficit hyperactivity disorder; his need to be constantly moving or drumming and his sometimes frank comments put him at odds with peers and teachers. Ms. Young counseled the student to consider how his actions affected others, and she reinforced with the rest of the class that all students should be accepted. "By the end of the year, students came to see that he was smart and had specific talents and interests," she notes. "Empathy is the foundation for a positive classroom environment."

Another benefit of explicit instruction on teamwork and empathy is that discussing lesson content with their peers can help students better evaluate their own understanding of the material, and hearing other students' explanations of new concepts may help clarify some aspects of the lesson. One study indicates that peers can sometimes be better predictors than students themselves of their likely performance on tests (Helzer & Dunning, 2012), so studying and reviewing lessons in a group setting may give students a more realistic view of their current competencies and need for additional learning.

Teaching with Self-Monitoring in Mind

Returning to the metaphor of metacognition as a means for students to drive their brains toward academic success, teachers can introduce the concept of self-monitoring their learning to students by suggesting that they regularly consider the question, "How well am I driving my brain?" Explain that just as drivers can get tickets for violating traffic laws, students can miss valuable opportunities for learning if they don't steer their brains in the right direction and pay attention to useful signs along the way. Figure 6.1 offers an engaging way to illustrate how students can make the most of learning through self-monitoring as they drive their brains.

FIGURE 6.1

Tips for Self-Monitoring as You Drive Your Brain Car for Learning Success

Driving offenses:	Here's how to drive your brain for learning:
Inattentive driving	Just as drivers who get distracted behind the wheel may get lost or drive past their destination, learners need to pay attention to lessons and learning activities. Consider questions like these: • Am I on the right track for learning? • Do I need to stop and ask for directions or more information? • Do I need to adjust how I am driving my brain? • What is my destination for learning? How will I know when I am there?
Speeding	Just as a speedometer helps drivers maintain a safe speed, monitoring can help students make sure they're not driving their brains too fast for learning conditions. • Do I need to slow down and review this information? • Should I practice this new knowledge or skill to make sure I understand it before moving on?

(continued)

FIGURE 6.1   *Continued*

Tips for Self-Monitoring as You Drive Your Brain Car for Learning Success

Driving offenses:	Here's how to drive your brain for learning:
Failure to yield	Just as traffic signs help drivers navigate safely, following directions for classroom assignments and tests and working well with others can help students get where they need to go in learning. • Do I understand the directions? Am I following them correctly? • Am I interacting courteously and respectfully with my teacher and fellow students? • Do I listen well to what others have to say? • When we work together, what can I learn from other students about this lesson?
Making a wrong turn	Just as drivers occasionally miss a turn, especially when they're taking a new route, learners need to make sure they're heading in the right direction toward understanding. • How can I double-check my work? • How does this new information connect with what I already know about this subject? • Do I need additional information? • If I'm getting lost in this lesson, how can I get back on track? • Are there different ways of thinking about this information or solving this problem?
Poor maintenance	Just as cars need proper fuel and regular maintenance to keep running, students have more learning success when they monitor to make sure they are fueling their brains and bodies properly. • Am I fueling my brain with healthy foods? • Am I staying hydrated? • Is it time for an exercise break? • Am I getting enough sleep?

The Usefulness of Cognitive Flexibility

Here's a fun way to introduce the concept of cognitive flexibility to students. You'll need a shoe or small case with a Velcro closure, a Slinky spring, and chocolate chip cookies.

Step 1. Open and close the Velcro closure, and ask students how they use this invention in their everyday lives. Explain that it was invented by a man named George DeMestral, who was inspired by investigating how cockleburs stuck to his dog's fur. Today, Velcro closures are used in homes, in businesses, and even in space: when astronauts play chess, the pieces are kept on the board using the hook-and-loop fasteners.

Step 2. Juggle a Slinky spring back and forth in your hands, and ask how many students have played with this toy. Explain that the Slinky spring was invented accidentally in the 1940s by a mechanical engineer named Richard James who wanted to know how to keep sensitive ship equipment in place on the rolling seas.

Step 3. Pass around chocolate chip cookies and share one story of how they may have been invented. A woman named Ruth Wakefield owned a toll house in Boston, where travelers would stop to pay road tolls and have a meal. One day, Ruth wanted to make chocolate cookies for her guests but she had run out of cocoa. So she broke up a chocolate bar and mixed it into the cookie batter, thinking the chocolate would melt as the cookies baked. But instead an even yummier cookie, which became known as the toll house cookie, was invented!

Step 4. Note that these stories are about accidental creations, in which the inventors were thinking about something else but realized that their discovery could be useful in different ways. Explain that in the same way, we can all learn better by using flexible thinking, or *cognitive flexibility*. Cognitive flexibility allows us to look at things differently—to learn new ways of doing things and solve problems.

Step 5. Share examples of cognitive flexibility that resonate with students: A family taking a weekend trip runs into road construction and has to find a new way to get to their destination. A child turns a building set for a racecar into a cool robot. When it rains all weekend, the plans for a bike ride evolve into creating an obstacle course in the basement. Ask students to share their own examples of using flexible thinking to turn a setback into an opportunity.

Step 6. Explain that in the same way we can all use cognitive flexibility to help make learning easier:

- When you run into an unfamiliar word while reading, like *collaborate,* you can use flexible thinking to break it down into smaller, more familiar words. You know *co* means "together" and *labor* means "work," so this word might mean work together.

- When you're having a hard time remembering a long list of facts, you can think of different ways to increase recall, like using memory pegs or making up a song.

- When you get stuck on a tough math problem, think about different ways you might solve it. Consider this word problem: Sam buys 1.75 pounds of nails, 2.5 pounds of screws, 12 ounces of bolts, and 4 ounces of washers. What is the total weight of his purchase? To solve this problem, you could (a) convert all the weights to pounds and add them, (b) convert all the weights to ounces, add them, and divide by 16 to get the total pounds, or (c) add the total weight of the nails and screws in pounds and then, separately, add the total weight of bolts and washers, convert that number into the equivalent in pounds, and add it to the first number.

- When you can't decide how to start a writing assignment, focus instead on how you're going to organize the middle of the paper and what conclusion you want to make. When you go back, the introduction may be much easier to write.

- When the class is discussing a reading or history assignment, listen closely to what the teacher and other students say. You might hear something that makes you think, "I never thought about it that way before!" That different view can help make the lesson clearer.

Step 7. Look for opportunities to remind students when cognitive flexibility is useful—when a student solves a problem in an unexpected way, for example, or when a field trip gets canceled and the class ends up having a different learning experience.

Understanding Different Points of View

Guiding students to understand and respect other people's points of view can help foster a more positive learning environment and help them in their relationships at home, with friends, and in their future careers. To introduce this asset, try the following steps:

Step 1. Ask students to think about a time when they did not feel understood. You might share a personal example or an example from a story the class has been reading. Discussions about works of fiction are especially useful in exploring different perspectives because they provide rare insights into other people's thinking and emotions.

Step 2. Share the "six or nine" cartoon (see Figure 6.2) with students, and ask them to articulate what is causing the disagreement.

Step 3. Lead a discussion about why people have different points of view about things. Elaborate on contributions from students to emphasize that we are all unique, the sum of varied life experiences and family backgrounds. Remind students that our brains are as individual as our fingerprints, so we have different thoughts and opinions. Understanding and appreciating that others have different points of view makes life more interesting, and these differing perspectives can aid learning when we see lessons and problem solving in new ways.

Step 4. Encourage students to consider these questions when talking with others and when studying people from different times and places:

- What do other people see from where they are?
- How am I different from this person? How are we alike?

FIGURE 6.2

Conflict in Point of View

- How might this person's ideas make me think differently about mine?
- How can I show the same respect for others and their ideas that I expect from them?

Introducing Self-Monitoring

To help introduce the concept of self-monitoring to students, we suggest using the following ideas:

Explain that to achieve success in school and in life, it's important to monitor your progress. Exams are only one measure of how well you've learned—and you'll get a better grade if you monitor your learning along the way.

Emphasize that self-monitoring should cover the lesson content and their use of cognitive assets to enhance their learning. Here are examples of key questions: Do I understand this lesson? What are the most important things to know and remember about this lesson? What thinking skills can I use to make sure I am learning and to learn more effectively? Am I focusing my attention on learning? How can I transfer what I am learning in other subjects and settings?

Build in regular opportunities for students to check in on their developing knowledge during a lesson. Asking for a group or individual response to a quick question keeps students engaged, reinforces the concept, and gives students the opportunity to consider, "Do I know the answer?" (Schell, Lukoff, & Mazur, 2013).

Assign students to work in pairs or small groups and remind them that they can teach and learn from each other. Partners or groups may talk about the lesson in ways that make it more memorable or easier to understand. In addition, students will remember the lesson more easily and be able to apply it in other situations after explaining what they have learned to others. A key aspect of monitoring their learning is to strive to make the most of their interactions when working in groups.

Lesson: Switching Gears

Level: Kindergarten

Young students need regular opportunities throughout the school day for active play and learning. Incorporating active transitions or using songs between lessons and reminding students to direct their attention to a new subject helps to convey the message that they are in charge of monitoring and focusing their brains on learning. The concept of an *attention span* is familiar to teachers, but it may be more helpful to think about children's ability to focus on learning tasks as an *attention cycle* because even during a relatively brief lesson of 15 minutes, students' attention may ramp up and down (Wilson & Conyers, 2013b). Transition from one learning activity to the next can help gear up students' attention cycles so that they can more successfully maintain their focus on lessons.

Step 1. End a lesson or activity by emphasizing an important message about their learning to take advantage of the typically highest levels of attention at the beginning and end of an activity (known, respectively, as primacy and recency).

Step 2. Lead the children in a brief movement or musical break. Examples include a song based on the lesson set to a familiar tune (such as "Triangles, Circles, and Squares," in which children make the shapes with their arms as they sing to the tune of "Head and Shoulder, Knees and Toes") or a sorting game ("Everyone wearing a red shirt goes to this corner, everyone wearing a blue shirt goes to that corner."). A fun song to introduce lessons on letters might be set to the tune of "London Bridge": "Letters are such useful things, useful things. They help us spell our names and sing. We love letters!" Add a physical element by instructing students to form a letter with their body at the end of the song—something different every day, such as the first letter of their first or last names or the letter that begins the name of their favorite animal.

Step 3. Introduce students to the next lesson or activity by sharing an important concept they will learn, to take advantage of the primacy of their attention. Remind students that it is now time to focus their brains on learning.

Step 4. Throughout the lesson, check in with quick questions about the content so that children can monitor their learning.

Extender. Maureen Ryan, who teaches health and physical education at Jasper County Middle School in Georgia, shares strategies with her students on monitoring their focus on learning. She keeps a stationary bike in her classroom and students have the option to take turns pedaling and reading without disrupting the instructional flow. That option is useful for students who have a hard time just sitting at their desks.

Lesson: Monitoring Reading Comprehension

Level: Grade 5

Monitoring comprehension as students read independently is a common and vital aspect of metacognition in action for students. Teachers can share this checklist with all students in a class discussion and refer to it when working with individual students to underscore the strategies available for strengthening their reading skills (Wilson & Conyers, 2011b, p. 119). This checklist includes several of the cognitive assets presented in this text.

Before Reading

☐ I have established my clear intent by identifying what I want to achieve by reading this selection.

☐ I begin to make meaning from the book's title and introduction.

☐ I scan the text for what stands out (e.g., subtitles, key words, illustrations, boxed features, and guiding questions).

☐ I look for cues and make inferences to predict what I think will happen.

While Reading

☐ I connect key information in the text to what I know.

☐ I make notes about important details.

☐ I write questions about what I read that makes me curious or that I don't understand.

☐ As I read, I try to understand the author's point of view and the time and place of the text setting.

☐ I try to figure out the meaning of unfamiliar words based on the context of the passage.

Rereading

☐ I reread passages that I am curious about or didn't understand after reading the selection.

☐ I look up unfamiliar words in the dictionary and reread the passage to see if it has the same meaning I thought it had the first time around.

Summarizing

☐ I review the who, what, when, where, why, and how in this passage.

☐ I identify the most important elements of the text that convey its meaning.

☐ I paraphrase, or use my own words, to summarize the main elements of the text.

Evaluating

☐ What are my thoughts about this text?

☐ How do I feel about what I've read?

☐ Who else can I talk to about what I've read?

☐ I review my clear intent. Did I get what I intended from this reading? Why or why not?

☐ What do I plan to do with what I've read? Can I apply it in school or in my life outside school?

Lesson: Mix-It-Up Math

Level: Middle School

A useful message is that there's no single right way to solve a math problem. An educator's practice guide on *Teaching Strategies for Improving Algebra Knowledge in Middle and High School Students* (Star et al., 2015) recommends teaching students to identify and employ alternative strategies when solving algebra problems. In class and small group discussions, encouraging students to share and explain the reasoning behind different ways at arriving at a solution can help clarify fundamental math concepts.

Consider this common example: Let's say your bill for dinner is $12, and you want to leave a 15 percent tip. How much will you pay in total? One way to solve this problem is to multiply $12 by 1.15 to get $13.80. Or you might be able to work the problem more easily in your head by thinking: 10 percent of $12 is $1.20, and half of that is 60 cents, so 15 percent is $1.80. Add that to $12 and you get $13.80.

For more complex problems, Star and colleagues suggest introducing each strategy and giving students an opportunity to practice it before introducing another strategy for solving the problem. Once students are familiar with multiple strategies, ask two or more students to show their work using the different strategies and then explain their work. Emphasize that if students have a hard time using one strategy, they can switch to another one. Understanding multiple strategies also offers students options for double-checking their work. These reflective questions can help students monitor their choice and use of different math strategies:

- What strategies could I use to solve this problem? How many possible strategies are there?

- Of the strategies I know, which seems to best fit this particular problem?

- Is there anything special about this problem that suggests that a particular strategy is or is not applicable or a good idea?

- Why did I choose this strategy to solve this problem?

- Could I use another strategy to check my answer? Is that strategy sufficiently different from the one I originally used? (Star et al., 2015, p. 30)

Extender. Younger students can also be taught to monitor their math skills by using two or more strategies to solve a problem and double-check their work. For example, a 2nd grader may rely on rote memory to answer that $7 + 4 = 11$, but she can double-check her answer by subtracting 4 from 11 or using a number line.

Lesson: Homework "Wrappers"

Level: High School

Lovett (2008) introduced the concept of "wrappers" as a learning activity to surround classroom lectures and discussions, assignments, projects, and assessments with a metacognitive mindset. Wrappers are simple questions teachers can pose to guide students to monitor and assess their learning progress and the effectiveness of the strategies they use while learning. To introduce homework wrappers use the following steps:

Step 1. Hand out sheets explaining the homework assignment with a wrapper question at the beginning: "This assignment is about _____. How quickly and easily can you complete _____?" Then include the instructions for the assignment. At the end of the homework sheet, add some concluding wrapper questions: "Now that you have completed the assignment, was it easier or harder than you expected? What cognitive assets you learned in class helped with this assignment? What worked and didn't work? What might you do differently the next time you have an assignment like this?"

Step 2. Lead a classroom discussion on the assignment, including the wrapper questions. Focus the discussion on how questions like these can help students monitor and improve their learning. Ask students to share their responses to the wrappers. In Lovett's work with college students (2008) on vector arithmetic homework, some responses included "I realized that I was a little slow at subtracting vectors, and now I understand it better and can find the difference more quickly" and "At the beginning of the exercise, I was more confident in using vectors than I probably should have been."

Step 3. Over time, fade the explicit inclusion of wrapper questions by moving from including them in written homework descriptions to reminding students verbally to monitor how well they worked on the assignments and which strategies were useful. Continue to emphasize the importance of monitoring their thinking and use of cognitive assets as they work independently and with other students. Wrappers are a seemingly simple tool, but Lovett notes that "research shows even minor interventions that frame a task in a new way can significantly change behavior," such as using new strategies to aid in learning.

Metacognition Checkpoint

Encourage students to be metacognitive about monitoring their learning and productive interactions with others by considering questions like these:

- How is my learning going?
- What have I learned so far? What do I still need to learn?
- How does what I'm learning connect with what I already know?
- Do I need to adjust my thinking?
- How well am I doing in developing this new skill?
- Am I following the directions for this assignment or assessment?
- Is there more than one way to solve this problem?
- Have I double-checked my work?
- Can I explain what I have learned to others?
- What can I learn from other students when they explain the lesson content to me?

 ## Self-Monitoring in Your Professional Practice

The same strategies that can help students monitor their learning, tackle tough problems by applying cognitive flexibility, and make the most of learning with their peers can also assist teachers in honing their instructional practice:

Monitoring student learning. Standards developed by the National Council of Teachers of English (2013), which are applicable across subjects, recommend ways to weave formative assessment into everyday lessons to monitor students' understanding and application of their developing knowledge as they learn, not just when the unit is complete. This metacognitive approach to monitoring students' progress entails

  • Providing immediate, actionable feedback to facilitate the most productive next steps toward learning success;

  • Emphasizing steady progress and acknowledging incremental gains;

  • Guiding students to set and work toward learning goals and intentions; and

  • Reminding students to monitor what is and isn't working as they learn.

Applying cognitive flexibility. When an unexpected event or an unforeseen turn in a classroom discussion takes the learning in a new direction, are you flexible enough to set aside your lesson plans and follow that lead? Teachers must adapt continually in managing the learning and behaviors of a room full of diverse students by recognizing teachable moments and responding to the needs of students to slow down, speed up, or approach learning from a different direction. Cognitive flexibility is an approach much in demand in making the more than one thousand decisions that regularly arise in a single day of teaching (Kauchak & Eggen, 2013).

Understanding others' points of view. Students become more empathetic and respectful of their peers' perspectives and ideas when their teacher models those behaviors. Are all students encouraged to share their points of view? Do you acknowledge students' feelings about learning, even when they are frustrated or bored? When students' attention begins to stray, it might be a good time for a brief activity break or to switch gears with a different learning activity. When students exhibit frustration, teachers can respond empathetically by noting that learning can be hard work and guiding students to back up and try other learning and problem-solving strategies. Above all, keep in mind that as students become more empathetic, they will more consistently reflect the emotional pitch of their learning environment, so it is up to you as lead learner to model an optimistic and positive outlook.

Staci Berry, general studies principal at Rohr Middle School in North Miami Beach, Florida, says adopting a metacognitive approach to education means that she is "always evaluating and thinking about how I can say something better, how I can get better results, and how I can inspire teachers to take these ideas into their classrooms." During the 2013–14 school year, Ms. Berry learned a great deal as a member of two learning communities—at her school and among a group of teachers earning their graduate degrees:

> Both communities have inspired me, enlightened me, and helped me strengthen my mission. At the same time, I have grown just as much through the challenges I have been given to use metacognition to complete each of my course requirements. Having not been a student for many years, the learning curve was steep, but with each small success, and with every vote of confidence from my professors and cohorts, I gained more practical optimism, clear intent, and finishing power that kept me focused and determined to succeed. I definitely adopted a growth mindset. Effort, hard work, and persistence, not intelligence, have driven my success. (Personal correspondence, January 23, 2015)

7

Start and Finish Strong with Metacognition

To help students become wise learners, teachers can guide them to view mistakes as "the stuff of learning"—golden opportunities for self-reflection and improvement. The cognitive asset of *learning from experience* involves students reflecting on the outcomes of academic assignments and tests to assess how well they did, what strategies were most helpful in achieving learning goals, and what they might do differently in the future to improve performance. The goal is not to eliminate mistakes but to learn from them so they are not repeated. Through explicit instruction and modeling by their teacher and regular practice on their own, students can learn the mechanics and benefits of applying a metacognitive approach to learning from their experiences. Students can easily apply this approach across subjects and in their future academic, career, and personal endeavors.

A related cognitive asset is *finishing power*—appropriate task completion that is sustained over time and in spite of difficulty (Wilson & Conyers, 2011b). Many students begin assignments and projects with high aspirations, but over time their enthusiasm wanes as other commitments and distractions claim their attention. Teachers can cultivate finishing power in their students' approach to learning through explicit instruction and modeling of the importance of finishing what you start.

Finishing power relies on the use of other cognitive assets along the way: establishing clear intent, developing and following a systematic plan, monitoring progress and revising one's plans along the way when necessary, and maintaining practical optimism that success is possible through hard work and persistent effort. Students can cross the finish line to academic success when they drive their brains by applying a metacognitive approach to the entirety of learning activities.

Teaching with Learning from Experience and Finishing Power in Mind

To introduce younger children to the importance of learning from experience, share the tales of storybook characters who try and struggle, rethink their strategies, and try again until they accomplish their goals. For example, in Ashley Spires's *The Most Magnificent Thing* (2014), the protagonist persists through feeling frustrated and discouraged to achieve her creative aim.

For older students, it might be helpful to start with a familiar or personal example, such as this: "I have a problem. It seems like every morning I end up searching for my car keys. Does anyone have any ideas about how I could solve that?" Students may come up with several possible solutions that come down to leaving them in the same, visible location every evening. Thank students for their suggestions. A few days later, mention that this solution has really worked well. In fact, it's a great example of learning from experience by thinking about how to correct a mistake and taking positive action.

Next, ask students for other examples of how they or people they know have learned from experience. Guide the discussion toward learning from experience to improve their grades and to make the metacognitive and cognitive strategies they use in learning more effective. Emphasize that the mistakes they make on tests and in learning projects are opportunities to learn and improve. Share examples like these and ask students to suggest some of their own:

- "I used subtraction to solve this problem when I should have used multiplication. The next time I will double-check to make sure I used the best method to solve the problem."

- "I ran out of time to answer all the questions. The next time I will go past the tricky questions that may take a lot of time and answer all the rest. Then I'll go back and answer the harder ones."

- "The science team that won the challenge match had a really great strategy for quickly brainstorming and agreeing on the best answer. Our team should try that."

- "This was the first time I relied on my outline to organize and write my paper. It turned out really well. I'm going to use an outline for every paper I write."

Explain that learning from experience entails thinking about what went well and what didn't in learning and studying. People who learn from experience don't get mad at themselves when they make a mistake; they just figure out how not to repeat it. But learning from experience is not just about correcting mistakes. It's also about paying attention to what helps you succeed, so you can continue to get better.

Conclude your introduction on a proactive approach to learning from experience by stressing that this example of being metacognitive can help everyone in every age and stage. Lots of people benefit from learning from experience: Athletes and musicians learn how to improve their techniques by thinking about their practice and performance. Workers aim for continuous improvement in their business by looking for ways to produce goods more quickly and with fewer mistakes. Cooks sometimes experiment with recipes to improve them; when the results of those experiments are not edible, they know what not to do next time!

Finishing Power

Start only what you plan to finish. Finish what you start. These are powerful messages for students of all ages. To introduce the cognitive asset of finishing power before launching an assignment for an individual or group learning project, try the following:

Step 1. Tell students they will be beginning a big project. To succeed in this assignment, they will need to start strong *and* finish strong.

Step 2. Note that starting something new is exciting. Many people start a new project with great enthusiasm, but along the way, they lose steam. They might run into problems or get distracted by other tasks.

Step 3. Explain that a great idea is useless if you don't follow through with finishing power. Middle school teacher Therese Reder introduces this cognitive asset by sharing a PowerPoint presentation with her students depicting how impractical bridges, houses, cabinets, and boats are if they are left unfinished. She then relates that idea to the need for students to persist until they finish their projects.

Step 4. Emphasize that to finish strong on their projects, students will need to use other cognitive assets they have learned:

• Establish their clear intent for the project and regularly check back to make sure they are working toward that goal.

• Develop a systematic plan and follow each step in that plan on schedule.

• Monitor their progress and decide if they need to revise their plan along the way.

• Maintain their optimism that they will succeed if they work hard and stay focused on executing their plan to achieve their clear intent.

Step 5. After introducing the learning project, regularly remind students that they will need to stay strong to finish strong!

Step 6. At the end of the project, tell students that finishing power is worth celebrating. Then offer an appropriate reward for their hard work, perhaps an extra-long recess for younger students or a favorite activity for older students.

Step 7. When students come back together, conclude with the message that finishing power will serve them well throughout their years in school and in their other pursuits. The commitment to develop clear intent, to devise and execute an action plan, and to carry it out to a strong finish is a true formula for success worth celebrating.

Introducing Learning from Experience and Finishing Power

To encourage students to develop their abilities to learn from experience and employ finishing power, we suggest using the following ideas:

Explain that tests provide one method of assessing how well students have learned lesson content, but there are other ways they can drive their brains to improve learning. They can consider whether their test-taking strategies helped them do better. They can ask themselves whether they studied long enough and whether the memory strategies they used were helpful.

Look for opportunities to model learning from experience and to emphasize when students are using this cognitive strategy in a useful way.

Remind students that a strong finish to their assignments and projects begins with developing a good plan and monitoring their progress along the way.

Give options—in addition to formal assessments and required tests, give students options to demonstrate and apply what they have learned by completing projects of their choice that extend the learning.

Provide formal tools to guide students to learn from experience such as checklists to assess their performance on an assignment or project or an adaptation of homework wrappers (see Chapter 6) to sharpen students' metacognitive focus on their test-taking performance and abilities.

Lesson: "The Next Time" Strategy for Writers

Level: Elementary

Teacher Marcy McIver (2013) developed a lesson based on two learning strategies, success mapping and the next time (TNT) (Wilson & Conyers, 2011a), to guide her 3rd grade class in a private school in Dubai to improve their writing skills. Ms. McIver had noted that her students were making the same writing errors repeatedly, mistakes they could correct if they learned to review and edit their work. By introducing these strategies, her goal was to help students improve their *procedural knowledge*—a practical understanding of how they can apply their writing strengths and improve their weaknesses and why it is important to stay focused on achieving their targeted goals.

Step 1. Set students on a positive trajectory by emphasizing that they have the ability to become better writers. Success mapping involves developing a concrete approach for students to reflect on what they have achieved to maintain a positive momentum for the next learning challenge. Ms. McIver created a graphic organizer in the form of a success ladder to guide students to chart their progress in developing their writing skills. On each rung of the ladder, students write a rule that they have used successfully in their assignments, such as "end each sentence with a period," "use capital letters for names and the first word of a sentence," and "add adjectives to make my writing more detailed." The success ladder is intended to reinforce their improvement as writers by adhering to these rules and to remind them to use all the rules when they edit their first drafts.

Step 2. Guide students to create their own personal writing goals based on the rules they are learning for each assignment. Ms. McIver hands out laminated bookmarks with a colorful TNT label so each student can write their target goal on the bookmark with a whiteboard marker. Students keep their target bookmark with their writing notebook so they can review it regularly and apply the goal to their writing.

Step 3. Initially, remind students regularly with explicit instructions and modeling to check in with their success ladders and TNT goals to ensure they are applying those rules to their writing. Ms. McIver also builds peer learning and collaboration into writing instruction by assigning students to review each other's writing and remind their fellow students about the rules of writing.

Step 4. Over time, give fewer reminders as students routinely apply the rules of writing and use their success ladders and TNT markers to set and achieve their goals.

Ms. McIver conducted an action research project employing the success ladder and TNT strategies over four weeks in her classroom. The rate of students being able to identify their targeted goals to use specific rules of writing increased from 11 percent to 95 percent in that period, and the rate of students applying the targeted rules independently increased from 5 percent to 87 percent. In addition, their teacher identified an improvement in students' procedural knowledge. In assessments about using these strategies, students demonstrated an increasingly metacognitive approach to their writing with responses such as "It helped me think about what I can do and what I can work on" and "It helped me think about what I already know." In formal writing assessments, students' performance improved from 56 percent to 78 percent after learning to employ these strategies.

Extender. The strategies of success mapping and guiding students to consider how to improve their writing the next time they write a paper or report are useful for older students as well. Students could keep a success folder of writing assignments where they did a good job progressing from outline to first draft to polished final draft as a reminder of the steps of good writing. TNT offers a simple reminder to students to review what went well and what they might do differently in future assignments.

Lesson: Metacognitive Approach to Assessment

Level: High School

As the high school students in Michael Fitzgerald's English class conclude their studies of a Shakespearean play or other literature, they must complete a preassessment of each act or book section to test their understanding of the plot and characters. Then the *real* assessment begins, as students take charge of demonstrating and applying what they have learned. They must earn three points by completing one to three projects of their choice:

• Their options for one-point projects include writing a diary entry for one of the characters in the play, imagining the advice that one character might offer another, or developing a 15-question quiz about the play.

• They can earn two points by taking a written test.

• Examples of assessment projects that would earn three points are writing a poem inspired by a theme in the play, writing and delivering a speech that delves deeper into a central idea, developing a schematic or visual art representation, scripting and drawing a five-panel comic strip inspired by the drama, or creating and presenting an interpretive performance of a scene not included in the play but related to it.

Mr. Fitzgerald notes that students have come up with some original ideas to complete these assessments. After the class read the book *Anthem* by Ayn Rand, one student was inspired by a character who rediscovers a way to power electric lights. The student designed a project to create his own battery-powered light using a potato; he also wrote a summary of the science behind his project.

The students' chosen assessments also must include a written component at the end that expounds on their projects. Then they grade their projects on a four-point scale to assess what they did well, where they might have fallen short, and how they might improve their performance in the future.

"At-risk kids are very hesitant to give themselves a four out of four, maybe because of a lack of validation about their abilities in the past," Mr. Fitzgerald says. "If they give themselves a three, that's what I give them. If they give themselves a two, I may give them more feedback about all the work they did and grade them up. This approach of assessing their own performance and how they might improve in the future instills in them a growth mindset."

This form of assessment entails a metacognitive approach to carry out their projects and evaluate them and requires students to employ many of the cognitive assets presented in this text. Students must establish their clear intent on how their projects will demonstrate their learning. They must plan carefully and manage their time, and they must put finishing power to work.

"Many students who struggle academically are bright and creative, but they haven't developed the forbearance to complete what they start," Mr. Fitzgerald says. "I tell students, 'If you start something, that's great. But if you don't finish it, it's useless. Throughout your life, if you start something, you have to finish it. The ability to see things through is the difference between successful people and unsuccessful people.'"

Metacognition Checkpoint

Encourage students to be metacognitive about learning from and applying their learning experiences by asking themselves questions like these:

- Am I on track with my plan to finish this project fully and on schedule?
- What obstacles do I need to overcome to finish this project?
- How will I feel in celebrating the completion of this project?
- Have I achieved my clear intent?
- What went well with this assignment, project, or test? How could I improve my performance the next time?

Learning from Experience to Enhance Your Professional Practice

Educators who are committed to a metacognitive approach to their instructional practice are constantly learning from experience and tucking new strategies into their teaching toolbox. Every term a new group of students enters the classroom, requiring teachers to approach every lesson, even if they have been teaching for years, with fresh eyes on how best to optimize learning for all students. To purposefully learn from experience—their own and those of fellow educators—teachers can

- Continually evaluate learning outcomes and instructional effectiveness, even in familiar lessons.

- Become avid readers of educational books, journals, and other resources.

- Actively participate in team meetings with colleagues, professional development sessions, and other opportunities for collaboration with peers.

- Contribute to and learn from online communities for educators.

- Volunteer to mentor and be mentored by colleagues and recognize that both teachers in these partnerships can grow professionally by sharing and reflecting on what works in their classrooms.

- Frequently consider the question, "What might I do differently next time so that I can continue to improve my teaching practice?" (Conyers & Wilson, 2016).

Next Steps Toward Metacognitive Teaching and Learning

Applied in combination and practiced until they become second nature, the metacognitive and cognitive strategies described in this text support a more proactive and effective approach to teaching and learning. Applying decades of educational research, we now know that a metacognitive mindset improves academic performance across core subjects and that the use of metacognitive and cognitive strategies is a key variable that sets successful students apart from peers. We also know that explicit instruction on how, why, when, and where to use these strategies benefits students across the range of current performance, from those identified as gifted to struggling learners. By wielding these cognitive tools, students can bolster their learning strengths and purposefully identify and strive to overcome weaknesses as they drive their brains to successful outcomes in school, in their personal pursuits, and in their future careers.

Figure 7.1 provides a simple checklist outlining the metacognitive and cognitive strategies we have presented to meet the diverse needs of a classroom of unique learners. One teacher described the positive symbiotic effect on her students' learning following explicit instruction on the use of these strategies: "My students are more optimistic, less stressed, and more cooperative. Because of this, they are better able to pay attention and engage with the lesson and the activities. As a result of higher engagement, they are learning and retaining more."

Middle school teacher Therese Reder uses verbal cues, posters and other visual reminders, and direct modeling and interaction to help students become more adept and comfortable using a variety of metacognitive strategies and cognitive assets in the classroom and in life. She also helps students identify and build on their learning strengths and preferences to establish their clear intent, set learning goals and establish plans to achieve them, and process and transfer their learning. As a result of putting this approach to work in her classroom, Ms. Reder says, "I've been able to diversify my strategies more effectively, student learning delved to deeper levels, and I found them more eager to keep trying rather than give up."

These perspectives from classroom teachers illustrate the gains that result from explicit instruction on the use of meta-

FIGURE 7.1

Metacognition in Action Checklist

How students exhibit their understanding and use of metacognition and cognitive assets in learning:	How often do students exhibit metacognition and cognitive assets?		
	Often	Sometimes	Not yet
Understanding metacognition: Explains in their own words the benefits of thinking about one's thinking to improve learning			
Exhibiting metacognition: Demonstrates mindfulness of their thinking and use of cognitive strategies, such as considering how to improve study habits, reading comprehension, writing and problem-solving skills, and performance on assessments			
Power of neuroplasticity: Demonstrates a basic comprehension that brain plasticity powers ability to learn and improve knowledge and skills			
Practical optimism: Exhibits a positive outlook about the likelihood of succeeding in learning as the result of purposeful and persistent effort			
Clear intent: Establishes and can readily state goals for assignments and learning activities			
Systematic planning: Develops and follows a specific plan and schedule to complete assignments and learning activities			

(continued)

FIGURE 7.1 *Continued*

Metacognition in Action Checklist

How students exhibit their understanding and use of metacognition and cognitive assets in learning:	How often do students exhibit metacognition and cognitive assets?		
	Often	Sometimes	Not yet
Selective attention: Focuses appropriately on learning tasks and listens carefully to teachers, peers, and other speakers			
Working memory: Independently employs strategies to make the most of "think space" in processing and analyzing relevant information to enhance understanding and recall of lesson content			
Self-monitoring: Regularly evaluates understanding and skill development while engaged in learning tasks such as reading, discussing lesson content, and solving problems			
Cognitive flexibility: Considers multiple options in problem solving, demonstrates ability to analyze complex ideas, and recognizes when it may be useful to adjust thinking and actions			
Understanding others' points of view: Shows respect for others' statements and opinions and is willing to consider other people's ideas			
Learning from experience: Proactively evaluates learning outcomes with a focus on how to improve in the future and apply/transfer new knowledge and skills			
Finishing power: Persists to complete tasks on schedule and in spite of difficulties or distractions that may arise			

cognition and cognitive strategies to help students drive their brains to optimize learning. When teachers begin the school year by introducing the concept and benefits of a metacognitive approach to learning and provide explicit instruction, guidance, and modeling throughout the year on developing cognitive assets, students may see the results of taking charge of their learning and the transformational potential of using what they have learned about metacognition in school and in life. Guiding students to become metacognitive in their learning is consistent with the primary aim of the Every Student Succeeds Act, which seeks to improve excellence and equity in all schools.

There is no one right way to teach students how to drive their brains for learning. This text covers a wide range of ideas and strategies for implementation that you can apply and adapt for your grade level, subject matter, and curriculum. In working with thousands of students to create our unique approach to teacher education and professional development, we have found that one of the most exhilarating experiences is when the light bulb of discovery switches on as students realize they are in charge of their learning and have the capacity to succeed. Teachers tell us they have felt this same excitement. The reward of seeing students "get it" and begin to use these powerful tools on their own taps into one of the prime motivations of why we teach—to help all of our students reach more of their learning potential.

References

Allington, R. L. (2011, August). What at-risk readers need. *Best of Educational Leadership 2010–2011, 68*(10), 40–45. Available at http://www.ascd.org/publications/educational_leadership/summer11/vol68/num10/What_At-Risk_Readers_Need.aspx

Alloway, T., & Alloway, R. (2013). *The working memory advantage: Train your brain to function stronger, smarter, faster.* New York: Simon & Schuster.

Amabile, T., & Kramer, S. J. (2011, May). The power of small wins. *Harvard Business Review.* Retrieved from https://hbr.org/2011/05/the-power-of-small-wins/ar/1

Anderman, E. M., & Anderman, L. H. (Eds.) (2009). *Psychology of classroom learning: An encyclopedia.* Farmington Hills, MI: Gale, Cengage Learning.

APA Division 15 Committee on Learner-centered Teacher Education for the 21st Century. (1995, November). Learner-centered psychological principles: Guidelines for the teaching of educational psychology in teacher education programs. *NEP/15 Newsletter for Educational Psychologists, 19*(1), 8.

Baker, L. (2013). Metacognitive strategies. In J. Hattie & E. M. Anderman (Eds.), *International guide to student achievement.* New York: Routledge.

Billings, L., & Roberts, T. (2012, December; 2013, January). Think like a seminar. *Educational Leadership, 70*(4), 68–72.

Bransford, J., Brown, A., & Cocking, R. (Eds.). (2000). *How people learn: Brain, mind, experience, and school* (Expanded ed.). Washington, DC: National Academies Press.

Bunce, D. M., Flens, E. A., & Neiles, K. Y. (2010, December). How long can students pay attention in class? A study of student attention decline using clickers. *Journal of Chemical Education, 87*(12), 1438–1443.

Cawelti, G. (2004). *Handbook of research on improving student achievement* (3rd ed.). Alexandria, VA: Educational Research Service.

Compton, W. C., & Hoffman, E. (2013). *Positive psychology: The science of happiness and flourishing* (2nd ed.). Belmont, CA: Wadsworth.

Conyers, M. A., & Wilson, D. L. (2015). *Positively smarter: Science and strategies to increase happiness, achievement, and well-being.* West Sussex, UK: Wiley Blackwell.

Conyers, M. A., & Wilson, D. L. (2016). *Smarter teacher leadership: Neuroscience and the power of purposeful collaboration.* New York: Teachers College Press.

Cowan, N. (2008). What are the differences between long-term, short-term, and working memory? *Progress in Brain Research, 169,* 323–338. Retrieved from http://www.ncbi.nlm.nih.gov/pmc/articles/PMC2657600/

Draganski, B., Gaser, C., Kempermann, G., Kuhn, H. G., Winkler, J., Buchel, C., & May, A. (2006). Temporal and spatial dynamics of brain structure changes during extensive learning. *The Journal of Neuroscience, 26*(23), 6314–6317.

Dunlosky, J. (2013, Fall). Strengthening the student toolbox: Study strategies to boost learning. *American Educator,* 12–21. Retrieved from https://www.aft.org/sites/default/files/periodicals/dunlosky.pdf

Dweck, C. S. (2006). *Mindset, the new psychology of success: How we can learn to fulfill our potential.* New York: Ballantine.

Efklides, A., & Misailidi, P. (Eds.). (2010). *Trends and prospects in metacognition research.* New York: Springer.

Ericsson, K. A., Prietula, M. J., & Cokely, E. T. (2007, July–August). The making of an expert. *Harvard Business Review.* Retrieved from http://141.14.165.6/users/cokely/Ericsson_Preitula_&_Cokely_2007_HBR.pdf

Feuerstein, R., Feuerstein, R. S., & Falik, L. H. (2010). *Beyond smarter: Mediated learning and the brain's capacity for change.* New York: Teachers College Press.

Flavell, J. H. (1976). Metacognitive aspects of problem solving. In L. R. Resnick (Ed.), *The nature of intelligence* (pp. 231–236). Hillsdale, NJ: Erlbaum.

Fleming, S. M. (2014, September/October). The power of reflection: Insight into our own thoughts, or metacognition, is key to higher achievement in all domains. *Scientific American,* 31–37.

Fotuhi, M. (2013). *Boost your brain: The new art and science behind enhanced brain performance.* New York: HarperOne.

Fredrickson, B. (2009). *Positivity: Groundbreaking research reveals how to embrace the hidden strength of positive emotions, overcome negativity, and thrive.* New York: Crown.

Germuth, A. A. (2012). *Helping all learners reach their potential: What teachers say about graduate programs that integrate the implications of education, mind, and brain research.* Winter Park, FL: BrainSMART.

Glaser, C. & Schlaug, G. (2003, October 8). Brain structures differ between musicians and non-musicians. *Journal of Neuroscience, 23*(27). Retrieved from http://www.jneurosci.org/content/23/27/9240.full

Goldberg, E. (2009). *The new executive brain: Frontal lobes in a complex world.* New York: Oxford University Press.

Good, T. L., & Brophy, J. E. (2008). *Looking in classrooms* (10th ed.). Boston, MA: Allyn & Bacon.

Greater Good Science Center, University of California, Berkeley. (n.d.). Empathy quiz. Retrieved from http://greatergood.berkeley.edu/quizzes/take_quiz/14

Green, A. (2015, April 27). The 10 most common interview questions: Study up to prepare a strong answer for each that highlights your skills and track record. *U.S. News & World Report Money.* Retrieved from http://money.usnews.com/money/careers/slideshows/the-10-most-common-interview-questions/1

Hacker, D. J., Dunlosky, J., & Graesser, A. C. (2009). *Handbook of metacognition in education.* New York: Routledge.

Harman, A. E., & Germuth, A. A. (2012). *Helping all learners reach their potential: What teachers say about graduate programs that integrate the implications of mind, brain, and education research.* Orlando, FL: BrainSMART.

Hartman, H. J. (Ed.). (2002). *Metacognition in learning and instruction: Theory, research and practice.* New York: Springer.

Hartman, H. J. (Ed.). (2010). *Metacognition in learning and instruction: Theory, research and practice* (Neuropsychology and Cognition Series, 2nd ed.). Norwell, MA: Kluwer.

Hattie, J. A. C. (2009). *Visible learning: A synthesis of over 800 meta-analyses relating to achievement.* New York: Routledge.

Hattie, J. A. C. (2012). *Visible learning for teachers: Maximizing impact on learning.* New York: Routledge.

Helzer, E. G., & Dunning, D. (2012, July). Why and when peer prediction is superior to self-prediction: The weight given to future aspiration versus past achievement. *Journal of Personality and Social Psychology, 103*(1), 38–53. doi: 10.1037/a0028124

Hinton, C., Fischer, K. W., & Glennon, C. (2012, March). Students at the center: Mind, brain, and education [Executive Summary]. Available at http://studentsatthecenter.org/sites/scl.dl-dev.com/files/field_attach_file/Exec_Hinton%26Fischer%26Glennon_032312.pdf

Jha, A. P., Stanley, E. A., Kiyonaga, A., Wong, L., & Gelfand, L. (2010). Examining the protective effects of mindfulness training on working memory capacity and affective experience. *Emotion, 10*(1), 54–64.

Kauchak, D. P., & Eggen, P. D. (2013). *Introduction to teaching: Becoming a professional* (5th ed.). Upper Saddle River, NJ: Pearson.

Killingsworth, M. A., & Gilbert, D. T. (2010, November, 12). A wandering mind is an unhappy mind. *Science, 330*(6006) 9320. doi: 10.1126/science.1192439

Kuhn, D. (2000). Metacognitive development. *Current Directions in Psychological Science, 9*(5), 178–181. Retrieved from http://www.mx1.education forthinking.org/sites/default/files/page-image/1-02Metacognitive Development.pdf

Lai, E. R. (2011, April). Metacognition: A literature review. *Pearson's Research Reviews.* Retrieved from https://moodle.elac.edu/pluginfile.php/111973/ mod_resource/content/0/Metacognition_Literature_Review_Final.pdf

Lickerman, A. (2013, June 30). How optimism can be learned: The answer isn't by aiming to be more optimistic. *Psychology Today.* Retrieved from https://www.psychologytoday.com/blog/happiness-in-world/201306/ how-optimism-can-be-learned

Lovett, M. C. (2008). Teaching metacognition (PowerPoint presentation). Retrieved from http://net.educause.edu/upload/presentations/ELI081/ FS03/Metacognition-ELI.pdf

Marzano, R. J. (2007). *The art and science of teaching: A comprehensive framework for effective instruction.* Alexandria, VA: ASCD.

Marzano, R. J., & Pickering, D. J. (2011). *The highly engaged classroom.* Bloomington, IN: Solution Tree Press.

Mayer, R. E. (2011). *Applying the science of learning.* Boston, MA: Pearson Education.

Mayer, R. E., & Wittrock, M. C. (2009). Problem solving. In E. M. Anderman & L. H. Anderman (Eds.), *Psychology of classroom learning: An encyclopedia* [Macmillan Social Science Library series] (pp. 702–706). Farmington Hills, MI: Gale, Cengage Learning.

McIver, M. (2013). TNT as a dynamite tool for improving writing [unpublished action research project]. Davie, FL: Nova Southeastern University, Fischler School of Education and Human Services.

Miller, D. C. (2007). *Essentials of school neuropsychological assessment.* Hoboken, NJ: Wiley.

National Council of Teachers of English. (2013). Formative assessment that truly informs assessment. Retrieved from http://www.ncte.org/positions/ statements/formative-assessment

National Governors Association Center for Best Practices [NGACBP] & Council of Chief State School Officers [CCSSO]. (2010a). *Common core state standards for English language arts and literacy in history/social studies, science, and technical subjects.* Available at http://www.corestandards.org

National Governors Association Center for Best Practices [NGACBP] & Council of Chief State School Officers [CCSSO]. (2010b). *Common core state standards for mathematics.* Available at http://www.corestandards.org

Nelson, A. C. H., & DuPuis, D. N. (2010). *The adventures of Super3: A teacher's guide to information literacy for grades K–2.* Santa Barbara, CA: Linworth.

Noomii. (2013, September 18). Happiness & career success [Infographic]. *The Un-Self-Help Blog,* September 18, 2013. Retrieved from http://www.noomii. com/blog/5104-happiness-career-success-infographic

Ogle, D. M. (1986). K-W-L: A teaching model that develops active reading of expository text. *The Reading Teacher, 40*(5), 564–570.

Pellegrino, J. W., & Hilton, M. L. (2012). *Education for life and work: Developing transferable knowledge and skills in the 21st century.* Washington, DC: National Academies Press.

Pianta, R., Belsky, J., Houts, R., & Morrison, F. (2007, March 30). Opportunities to learn in America's elementary classrooms. *Science, 315,* 1795–1796. doi: 10.1126/science.1139719

Pryce-Jones, J. (2012, November 25). Ways to be happy and productive at work. *The Wall Street Journal.* Retrieved from http://blogs.wsj.com/ source/2012/11/25/five-ways-to-be-happy-and-productive-at-work/

Rasmussen, H. N., Scheier, M. F., & Greenhouse, J. B. (2009, June). Optimism and physical health: A meta-analytic review. *Annals of Behavioral Medicine, 37*(3): 239–256. doi: 10.1007/s12160-009-9111-x

Schell, J., Lukoff, B., & Mazur, E. (2013). Catalyzing learner engagement using cutting-edge response systems in higher education. Retrieved from http:// mazur.harvard.edu/sentFiles/Mazurpubs_701.pdf

Schulman, P. (1999, Winter). Applying learned optimism to increase sales productivity. *Journal of Personal Selling and Sales Management, XIX*(1), 31–37. Retrieved from http://www.waldentesting.com/salestests/sasq/ SASQ%20article.PDF

Schwartz, B. (2013, September). Attention must be paid! *Slate.* Retrieved from http://www.slate.com/articles/life/education/2013/09/paying_attention_ is_a_skill_schools_need_to_teach_it.html

Seligman, M. E. P. (1998). *Learned optimism: How to change your mind and your life.* New York: Simon & Schuster.

Seligman, M. E. P. (2011). *Flourish: A visionary new understanding of happiness and well-being.* New York: Free Press.

Silvano, W. (2009). *Turkey trouble.* Tarrytown, NY: Marshall Cavendish.

Shonkoff, J. P., & Philips, D. A. (Eds.). (2000). *From neurons to neighborhoods: The science of early childhood development.* Washington, DC: National Academy Press.

Smith, J. (2013, January 11). How to ace the 50 most common interview questions. *Forbes.* Retrieved from http://www.forbes.com/sites/jacquelynsmith/2013/ 01/11/how-to-ace-the-50-most-common-interview-questions/

Spires, A. (2014). *The most magnificent thing.* Toronto, Ontario: Kids Can Press.

Star, J. R., Caronongan, P., Foegen, A., Furgeson, J., Keating, B., Larson, M. R., . . . Zbiek, R. M. (2015). *Teaching strategies for improving algebra knowledge in middle and high school students* (NCEE 2014-4333).

Washington, DC: National Center for Education Evaluation and Regional Assistance (NCEE), Institute of Education Sciences, U.S. Department of Education. Retrieved from the NCEE website: http://whatworks.ed.gov

Swenson, R. (2006). The cerebral cortex. *Review of clinical and functional neuroscience* (Chapter 11). Hanover, NH: Dartmouth Medical School. Retrieved from http://dartmouth.edu/~rswenson/NeuroSci/chapter.11.html

Sylwester, R. (1995). *A celebration of neurons: An educator's guide to the human brain.* Alexandria, VA: ASCD.

Sylwester, R. (2005). *How to explain a brain: An educator's handbook of brain terms and cognitive processes.* Thousand Oaks, CA: Corwin.

Szpunar, K. K., Moulton, S. T., & Schacter, D. L. (2013). Mind wandering and education: From the classroom to online learning. *Frontiers in Psychology.* Retrieved from http://www.ncbi.nlm.nih.gov/pmc/articles/PMC3730052/

Tavangar, H. (2014): Empathy: The most important back-to-school supply. Edutopia Social and Emotional Learning Blog. Retrieved from http://www.edutopia.org/blog/empathy-back-to-school-supply-homa-tavangar

Veenman, M. V. J., Hesselink, R. D., Sleeuwaegen, S., Liem, S. I. E., & Van Haaren, M. G. P. (2014). Assessing development differences in metacognitive skills with computer logfiles: Gender by age interactions. *Psychological Topics, 23*(1), 99–113.

Wang, M., Haertel, G., & Walberg, H. (1993). Toward a knowledge base for school learning. *Review of Educational Research, 63,* 249–294. doi: 10.3102/00346543063003249

Wilson, D. L. (1996a, February). The school psychologist as co-teacher and staff developer: A shift in thinking. *NASP Communique, 33*–34.

Wilson, D. L. (1996b). The school psychologist as co-teacher: An example using COGNET program as a means of teaching thinking skills. *Journal of Cognitive Education, 5,* 171–183.

Wilson, D. L., & Conyers, M. A. (2005). *Thinking for reading curriculum.* Orlando, FL: BrainSMART.

Wilson, D. L., & Conyers, M. A. (2011a). *BrainSMART: 60 strategies for increasing student learning* (4th ed.). Orlando, FL: BrainSMART.

Wilson, D. L., & Conyers, M. A. (2011b). *Thinking for results: Strategies for increasing student achievement by as much as 30 percent* (4th ed.). Orlando, FL: BrainSMART.

Wilson, D. L., & Conyers, M. A. (2013a). *Five big ideas for effective teaching Connecting mind, brain, and education research to classroom practice.* New York: Teachers College Press.

Wilson, D. L., & Conyers, M. A. (2013b). *Flourishing in the first five years: Connect implications from mind, brain, and education research to the developmen young children.* Lanham, MD: Rowman & Littlefield Education.

Wilson, D. L., & Conyers, M. A. (2014, October). The boss of my brain. *Educational Leadership, 72*(2). Retrieved from http://www.ascd.org/publications/educational-leadership/oct14/vol72/num02/%C2%A3The-Boss-of-My-Brain%C2%A3.aspx

Winne, P. H., & Azevedo, R. (2014). Metacognition. In R. K. Sawyer (Ed.), *The Cambridge handbook of the learning sciences* (2nd ed., pp. 63–87). New York: Cambridge University Press.

Wood, R. E., & Locke, E. A. (1987). The relation of self-efficacy and grade goals to academic performance. *Educational and Psychological Measurement, 47*(4), 1023–1024.

Woollett, K., & Maguire, E. A. (2011, December 20). Acquiring "the Knowledge" of London's layout drives structural brain changes. *Current Biology,* 2109–2114. Retrieved from http://www.ncbi.nlm.nih.gov/pmc/articles/PMC3268356/

Index

Note: An *f* following a page number denotes a figure.

About the Authors

Donna Wilson, leader of the academic team at BrainSMART and the Center for Innovative Education and Prevention, is an educational and school psychologist and former teacher. Donna is codeveloper of graduate studies in mind, brain, and education science at the master's through doctoral levels and has facilitated professional development with tens of thousands of educators. Some of her current projects include work in partnership with the Blue Ribbon Schools of Excellence; numerous speaking engagements with educational leaders, teachers, and policymakers across the United States; a countrywide implementation of BrainSMART® Teaching and Learning in Jamaica; and professional development engagements in various locations around the world. Her passion is supporting teachers and administrators by modeling practical strategies grounded in research on how people learn. To bring Donna to your district or state, contact her at donna@brainsmart.org. View her blog at http://donnawilsonphd.blogspot.com/ or connect with her on LinkedIn under Donna Wilson, Ph.D.

 **Marcus Conyers** is a doctoral researcher at the University of Westminster and director of research and development for the Center for Innovative Education and Prevention. He is the founder of BrainSMART and coauthor of 20 books on applying the science of learning. Marcus has led statewide initiatives and worked in 30 countries, reaching more than 100,000 administrators and teachers. He has presented at academic conferences at universities in the United States and Canada, at the University of Cambridge in the United Kingdom, and at Leiden University in the Netherlands. Beyond educational audiences, Marcus is committed to sharing practical applications on the benefits of becoming more metacognitive with professionals in business and government organizations. To bring Marcus Conyers to your organization contact him at marcus@brainsmart.org. View his website at http://www.innovatingminds.org/, his blog at Innovating Minds, and connect with him on LinkedIn.

Both **Donna Wilson** and **Marcus Conyers** are on the web at www.brainsmart.org. You can also find them on Facebook at BrainSMART and follow them on Twitter @BrainSMARTU and Pinterest at BrainSMARTU.

Related ASCD Resources: Brain and Teaching

At the time of publication, the following ASCD resources were available (ASCD stock numbers appear in parentheses). For up-to-date information about ASCD resources, go to www.ascd.org.

ASCD EDge® Group

Exchange ideas and connect with other educators interested in "Let's Talk the Brain and Learning" or "Brain Compatible Learn" on the social networking site ASCD EDge® at http://ascdedge.ascd.org/

PD Online® Courses

An Introduction to the Whole Child (#PD13OC009M)

Print Products

Activating the Desire to Learn by Bob Sullo (#107009)

Brain Matters: Translating Research into Classroom Practice, 2nd ed. by Patricia Wolfe (#109073)

The Brain-Compatible Classroom: Using What We Know About Learning to Improve Teaching by Laura Erlauer (#101269)

Memory at Work in the Classroom: Strategies to Help Underachieving Students by Francis Bailey and Ken Pransky (#114005)

The Motivated Brain: Improving Student Attention, Engagement, and Perseverance by Gayle Gregory and Martha Kaufeldt (#115041)

The Motivated Student: Unlocking the Enthusiasm for Learning by Bob Sullo (#109028)

Research-Based Strategies to Ignite Student Learning: Insights from a Neurologist and Classroom Teacher by Judy Willis (#107006)

Teaching to the Brain's Natural Learning Systems by Barbara K. Given (#101075)

Teaching with the Brain in Mind, 2nd ed. by Eric Jensen (#104013)

Understanding How Young Children Learn: Bringing the Science of Child Development to the Classroom by Wendy L. Ostroff (#112003)

For more information: send e-mail to member@ascd.org; call 1-800-933-2723 or 703-578-9600, press 2; send a fax to 703-575-5400; or write to Information Services, ASCD, 1703 N. Beauregard St., Alexandria, VA 22311-1714 USA.

ASCD's Whole Child approach is an effort to transition from a focus on narrowly defined academic achievement to one that promotes the long-term development and success of all children. Through this approach, ASCD supports educators, families, community members, and policymakers as they move from a vision about educating the whole child to sustainable, collaborative actions.

Teaching Students to Drive Their Brains:
Metacognitive Strategies, Activities, and Lesson Ideas
relates to the safe, engaged, supported, and challenged tenets.

WHOLE CHILD
TENETS

1 HEALTHY
Each student enters school healthy and learns about and practices a healthy lifestyle.

2 SAFE
Each student learns in an environment that is physically and emotionally safe for students and adults.

3 ENGAGED
Each student is actively engaged in learning and is connected to the school and broader community.

4 SUPPORTED
Each student has access to personalized learning and is supported by qualified, caring adults.

5 CHALLENGED
Each student is challenged academically and prepared for success in college or further study and for employment and participation in a global environment.